"Now, When I Was a Kid"

"Now, When I Was a Kid"

By

DON RODABAUGH

Published by Leathers Publishing
4500 College Blvd., Suite 310
Leawood, Kansas 66211
1/888/888-7696

A Leathers Publishing Production
4500 College Blvd.
Leawood, KS 66211
Phone: 1 / 888 / 888-7696

PREFACE

WHO AMONG US during our formative years has not heard this rather condescending and often irksome title phrase from well-meaning relatives wishing to impart to the younger generation the enormous obstacles to be surmounted, and the onerous tasks that had to be performed while growing up, as compared to the soft, gentle coddling of the younger generation? Undoubtedly, this has been going on ever since man crawled out of his cave and started maintaining his own place of abode. It also probably followed man's discovery and development of new tools and labor-saving devices which, to the older generation, appeared to make the work of making a living much easier for the next generation. They may not have considered the more complex living standards and competitive interactions faced by the younger generation.

It is the hope of the author of these pages that a true recounting of the trials and tribulations, joys and ecstasies of his childhood on a small farm in the Midwest will give his children, as well as succeeding generations, a better insight into the day- by-day experiences of the author's generation. Phrases and colloquialisms of the time and locale have been purposely used to lend authenticity and flavor to the stories.

Dedicated to
my son Mark and daughter Phyllis
who have many times endured
what may have seemed to them
the exasperating words of this title.

TABLE OF CONTENTS

Chapter 1

Discovering the World Around Me

I WAS TOLD I came into the world on a cold day in February in the year 1913, without the niceties of a hospital or even the services of a doctor. Undoubtedly the doctor must have arrived later to sort of tidy up the event, but 10 miles over dirt roads in the dead of winter is a bit far to expect immediate attention.

I was preceded in this family by two sisters and two brothers. In other words, I was the "baby of the family" and was frequently reminded of such for most of my childhood. My sisters, Vera and Minnie, were much older than I and were married and gone from the family nest before I was old enough to remember their being at home. They did, however, have a strong influence on my childhood since they lived close enough to our house to visit frequently, and I in turn got to visit in their homes. More will be told of those visits later.

My two brothers, Harold and Delmer (Del) were much nearer my age and had a great influence on my childhood. Harold was eight years older than I and was in high school by the time I started grade school. Consequently his activities were far different than mine, but he served as a role model for me and I was greatly influenced by his presence.

Del was only two years older than I and was equally influential in my development but more in the form of sibling rivalry. I was always the underdog in this relationship in both physical and mental competition. Two years makes a lot of difference in the developmental levels of a child. I wouldn't want to say I was intimidated by Del, but certainly I was kept in my place as the baby of the family.

Being born in the year '13 didn't bother me during my childhood because for the first five or six years of my life, I didn't know that number 13 was supposed to be unlucky. Perhaps my parents knew of this superstitious saying, but being of strong religious beliefs did or said nothing to further such devil-inspired nonsense. As a matter of fact, I didn't even know sin existed until I was old enough to visit the nearest town, which was approximately 10 miles away. This was because the community into which I was born was a closely knit, church-oriented group of people similar to the Mennonite sect, and rather closely guarded their children against any outside influences which might lead them into bad habits.

My father had come to this community from the state of Iowa because he had received some formal training in the ministry of his church and was selected to serve as a lay minister for the newly organized group. At that time it was customary for the lay ministers of the church to serve willingly and freely without any compensation for their time and effort in behalf of the church. That was all very noble and good, but it did not provide much help in maintaining the necessities for a family of five children. My father had to work very hard to try to "make ends meet" and at the same time prepare sermons for Sunday delivery, as well as perform wedding ceremonies, conduct funeral services and attend church meetings any day of the week.

My little 110-pound mother did her utmost to keep the family fed by growing a big garden, raising a flock of chickens and canning and preserving everything that grew in the garden and fruit orchard. This was in addition to cooking the meals, doing the laundry and cleaning the milk utensils. Being a little woman, she could not take long steps, so that in order to keep up with her work she had to go at sort of a little trot from one activity to another.

The house into which I was born was a big two-story wooden frame structure with 10-foot ceilings in both upstairs and downstairs rooms. It was an older house but was considered quite commodious by standards of the time. It had an imposing two-

story porch across the front with decorative support posts going first to the balcony of the upstairs, then proceeding on up to the roof. At one side of the house facing the road was a similar structure except that it was much smaller, providing entrance to the parlor downstairs and a balcony for a second-story bedroom.

The parlor was seldom used when I was growing up. I understand it was often used when my two older sisters were courting. There was even an old, very ornate organ that my sisters had learned to play, but I had neither the desire nor opportunity to study music sufficiently to learn to play the instrument.

Before we get away from the discussion of the structure of the house, I feel compelled to relate a traumatic experience I had with one of those high porches. I was just a little fellow, maybe five years old, when for some strange reason our parents had left my brother Del and I at home alone while they went to a church meeting of some sort. Del was always the bold, adventuresome type, and I suspect he had planned this stunt for some time. The idea was to climb up on the very top of our house and view the whole countryside from that perspective. This was his chance. I would have been happy to let him do it all by himself, but he was very insistent that I do likewise. I suspect he wanted someone to share the blame if our parents should come home earlier than expected.

The only way to get up on the roof was to go upstairs, go out on the top porch, shinny up a corner post and crawl out over the overhang of the roof to a flat tin roof above. Del made the climb in short order and yelled for me to come on up. I was quite reluctant to take the risk, but he dared me to do it. That was all it took. I climbed up the post and out over the edge of the roof just like a monkey. It was great fun running up the slope of the main roof to the very top of the house and viewing the neighbors' houses and breathing all that fresh air.

But then it came time to get down before our parents came home. Del lay down on his belly on the flat porch roof and squirmed out over the edge until he could grasp the supporting post with his bare feet. He quickly scrambled down the post and yelled for me to come on down. I too lay down on my belly and squirmed out far enough to get my legs over the edge of the eaves. But when I felt for the post with my feet, it wasn't there. My legs were just a few inches too short to reach the post, and there I hung approximately 20 feet from the ground and nothing under my feet except thin air. I was simply petrified. I had inched out as far as I felt was safe, and Del kept yelling for me to slide out a little farther and to hurry up or our folks might come home and catch us up there. I was torn between risking broken legs or the wrath of my parents coming

4

home and finding me up there. Finally in sheer desperation I inched out to a point of no return and swung my feet in and caught the post which supported me until I could scramble over the edge of the roof and down to safety. We never did tell our folks that we were ever up there, and I never had the desire to be up there again.

I have already mentioned the parlor where beaus were entertained by my older sisters. About the only other times the parlor was used was for weddings performed by my father, and when we were visited by some of our relatives from Iowa. I suppose this was for the purpose of showing our out-of-state relatives how refined we were by entertaining them in the most lavishly decorated room in the house.

A door from the parlor led into what we called the front living room. It, too, was mostly reserved for special occasions such as on Sunday when we had company after church, or if someone was sick and had to be given special attention. How well I remember when Del and I had the measles at the same time. The doctor said we had to stay cooped up in that room with the shades drawn for about 10 days. Toward the end of the incarceration and after the fever had gone down, we became quite trying for our mother. We fussed and quarreled almost constantly, and our mother had to stop what she was doing many times during the day to settle us down. The last straw came one day when our mother came in and caught Del hanging out the east window in bright sunshine petting our old dog lying on the porch. He had broken all the rules of the quarantine, so there was no further reason for keeping him in there. If he was going to be permanently blind for this infraction of the rules, he might just as well be turned loose to enjoy what time he had left. After it became apparent there were no immediate dire effects from his freedom, I too was allowed out of the room and for weeks afterward avoided going back into that room.

From the front living room one could go into the dining room which was primarily where we lived. There was a big old oak dining table which was the center of activity in our house.

It not only bore huge meals, especially when company came, but it also was a work bench for drawing pictures, playing with tinkertoys, making spool tractors and doing our homework from school. Homework was not often assigned in those days, the teacher preferring to have it done in the schoolroom during the day, but Del having discovered the world of books spent many hours poring over novels, assigned literary works and even the "Books of Knowledge" from our father's bookcase. I can vividly remember on cold winter nights seeing him perched on his knees in a chair with his elbows supporting his head and shoulders near the middle of the table where a smoky old kerosene lamp provided the only source of light.

Another memory of that table I had was the time my big brother Harold polluted my popcorn. We had just finished popping a big panful of popcorn with the old iron skillet on the kitchen stove, and the pan was brought into the dining room for the contents to be divided among us. Three equal piles of popcorn were placed on the table so each brother would have an equal share.

We were eagerly munching at our popcorn when Harold started slipping his hand over to my pile and grabbing a kernel of popcorn. Of course, I loudly objected to this and tried grabbing at some of his popcorn. After awhile we grew tired of this and Harold went out into the kitchen to get a drink of water. When he came back, he again started grabbing at my much diminished pile of popcorn. I hurriedly started eating the remainder of my popcorn so he wouldn't get any of the remaining kernels. Suddenly I experienced a horrible taste in my mouth and had to run to the kitchen to spit out the mouthful of corn. It was then I smelled the kerosene. Harold had dipped a grain of popped corn in kerosene when he supposedly went after a drink, then came back and slipped it into my pile while acting as if he was stealing my corn. Not being of a suspicious nature and more than a little gullible, I was to have many more tricks played on me by my big brothers.

The kitchen was my mother's workshop where she spent many long hours cooking up big bowls of beans, mashed potatoes, gravy, cornmeal mush and applesauce. The cornmeal mush was not eaten as such but was held over until the next morning when it was sliced and fried for breakfast. While this may not sound very appetizing, I assure you it was wonderful when covered with a generous supply of sorghum.

At least once a week my mother would bake four big loaves of "starter" bread, which meant the dough was mixed with a yeast preparation left over from last week's baking. The live yeast organisms were thus kept alive week after week and each time do their duty in making the bread "rise" before baking. We boys would usually manage to be hanging around close by when the bread came out of the oven, and that wonderful aroma of fresh-baked bread would draw us into the kitchen for a slice of the "heel" of the loaf richly spread with homemade butter. Kings could not have fared better.

Once in a great while, our mother would make what she called "jo-twisters." These were an unusual form of doughnuts which she had learned to make from her Dutch ancestry. I never did know what was put into them, but they were made from dough rolled out flat and cut into strips. Each strip was picked up and the ends pinched together to form a circle; then with a deft twist the circle would become two loops and the resultant figure dropped into a kettle of hot boiling grease. The dough would disappear into the bubbling liquid but in less than a minute reappear on the surface a much enlarged and swollen figure. It would soon turn to a beautiful golden color and was ready to be removed. It was immediately rolled into sugar and laid out to cool. Seldom was our mother able to accumulate more than a few of these because hungry boys were waiting for each one as it came out of the pot.

All this cooking my mother did was on an old coal and wood-fired range which required repeated attention. The fire would not hold overnight, so each morning before breakfast a fire had to be built and maintained all day long. The heat generated not only provided for cooking but warmed the kitchen as well. This was especially important in the winter when it came time for the Saturday night bath. We did not have a bathroom or running water in the house, so when it came our turn to take a bath we would go into the kitchen, open the oven door to let in more heat, dip out several gallons of hot water from the wash boiler on the stove and put it into a galvanized washtub for our bath. It was quite a trick to take a bath in those little round tubs. If you sat down in it, your feet had to stick out, and if your feet were in it, your rear end had to stick out. Needless to say, once a week was often enough to go through that ordeal.

In the summertime when a hot coal fire was unthinkable, there was a four-burner kerosene stove brought into use. It even had a tin oven that could set over two of the burners. Although this stove avoided heating up the kitchen, it was a poor substitute for the flavorful cooking of the old coal-fired range.

One of the most advanced labor-saving devices we had in the kitchen was a sink and pitcher pump. The pump drew water from a cistern underneath the house. Unfortunately, the water in the cistern was not fit to drink because it came from drainage off the roof of the house, and the roof was covered with old decaying cedar shingles. This resulted in the water being sort of an amber color with a musty odor. We were able to use the water for such things as filling the wash boiler to heat for baths and even to wash dairy utensils, providing we afterward rinsed them with scalding drinking water. The drinking water had to come from a deep well out in the yard, so we used it very sparingly to avoid extra trips out in the cold to pump another bucket of water. I think the greatest advantage to this in-house water system was having a sink into which my mother could pour waste water and not have to run outside with buckets of water. All our bath water, mop water and dishwashing water went through that sink to a spot out back of the kitchen. This system worked fine until the coldest days in the winter when the outside pipe would freeze up and not allow the water to come through. This had to be remedied by heating a stove poker to red hot and running outside to the back of the house and jamming the red hot poker into the frozen pipe. This might require two or three trips before we would finally get the drain opened up.

Not all waste water from the kitchen went through the sink. Any water that had food particles such as potato peelings, apple parings, bread crumbs and the like went into what was called a slop bucket. Every afternoon this bucket was carried to the hen house and poured into a large pan for the chickens to pick over. This was a great treat for the chickens and served as a garbage disposal for the household.

Getting back to a discussion of the house, there were four bedrooms in our house. One bedroom was downstairs just off the dining room, and that was where our parents slept. Very early in my life I too slept in that bedroom, but in a fold-out bed at the foot of my parents' bed. The only thing I could recall about that bed was that it was very uncomfortable. But I remember very vividly the move I eventually had to make to an upstairs bedroom.

To my mind there were all sorts of spooks, goblins and even bears up there in some of the closets. All this fantasy was aided and abetted by my older brothers who would even hide in the dark corners and jump out and yell "boo" as I came up the stairs. There were also very real scary things such as rats scrambling around in the walls and an old hoot owl that would fly to the top of our house and hoot at all the neighborhood owls. There were several occasions during my transition to the upstairs bedroom when I would wake up in the middle of the night, maybe after a scary dream, and imagine I heard something moving around under the bed or in the next room. I would come flying out of the bed and race downstairs, wake up my father and insist he come up and look.

There were three upstairs bedrooms, or maybe I should say three and a half, because there was sort of an open area at the head of the stairs that contained a bed in case we had more overnight guests than could be accommodated in the bedrooms. The bedroom that Del and I slept in was on the north side, and often in the wintertime we could see our breath when we got our heads out from under the covers in the morning.

As I mentioned before, there was no bathroom in the house, and the only toilet was a primitive two-holer out back of the hen house. As is generally known, small boys could seldom go through an entire night without having to relieve their bladder, but the very thought of having to jump out of bed on a cold night, run downstairs, out the back door to the privy behind the hen house was chilling to say the least. There was a north window in Del's and my bedroom that opened out to the back of the house. We figured it was a lot simpler to throw open that window and let go from that elevation to a spot behind the house. The greatest drawback to this solution was the shock of a cold north wind mixed with snow or rain dampening our relief. We never did tell the folks that we were using this shortcut, but if they had ever noticed, there was a big rusty spot on the galvanized roof of the kitchen just beneath our north window.

Of course, we did not require overnight guests to go through the discomfort of a trip to the privy in the middle of the night. The spare (guest) bedroom was equipped with a porcelain chamber (thunder mug) under the bed and even a taller enamel container with a lid, referred to as a slop jar, alongside the bed. I suspect my brother Harold would slip into the guest bedroom from his bedroom and use the slop jar, but I never did find out for sure.

Adjacent to our house and connected by a small porch was a building called the wash house. Naturally it was where the laundry was done, but it served numerous other purposes as well. The cream separator was located in the front section, and my father spent many hours turning the handle of that ingenious device of whirling cones and gears that would force the lighter butterfat portion to rise above the heavier skim milk, each coming out of a separate spout.

It was a common occurrence for the ever-present cats to come slipping into the room during the operation and start lapping at the skimmed milk pouring into the bucket on the floor. My father would yell "scat" and kick at the culprit, which very easily dodged the foot and retreated for a minute or two before sneaking back for another try. The cats eventually got more skimmed milk than they could drink, but it was always more exciting for them to steal it out of the bucket.

The wash house was also a place for taking baths in the summer when heat was not needed, processing meats in the winter, when we butchered hogs, and sometimes used as a second kitchen when it was necessary to fire up another kerosene stove to cook for threshers.

There were other outbuildings from the house such as a coal shed, a hen house, a brooder house and, of course, the privy which I have already mentioned. We also had a large barn and several attendant buildings which, along with the above outbuildings, will be described in the next chapter on chores.

Chapter II

Chore Time

PERHAPS THE GREATEST DIFFERENCE between the activities of children in modern times and those of my childhood was in the amount of work required of my generation in helping with the tasks of making a living for the family. These tasks were referred to as chores and were not exactly relished. Although we could not appreciate it at the time, these chores were an excellent means of teaching us responsibility and even a work ethic that carried over into our young adult lives.

Some of those chores were just plain drudgery in which it was difficult to see any future benefits, but they had to be done regularly for our immediate benefit. Such chores were those of daily carrying in several buckets of coal for keeping the fires going in the winter. There was also the business of going to the barn to pick up corn cobs for starting fires in the morning.

Usually the fire in the dining room stove was kept alive all night by covering the fire at bedtime with almost a bucketful of coal and shutting off all the dampers and drafts to keep it smouldering all night long. But fire in the kitchen range was allowed to go out every night and had to be restarted the next morning with dry cobs and kindling before we could have breakfast. Going after these cobs at the barn every evening and carrying in several buckets of coal were among my earliest chores, and I thoroughly detested doing them.

Every morning before daylight Del and I would be awakened by our father shaking down the ashes in the old coal-fired stove in the living room. This was immediately under our bedroom, and the harsh grating of the grates and the banging of the coal buckets was almost enough to wake up the dead. I'm satisfied our father didn't make any effort to lessen the noise because this was just part of the ritual of getting us out of bed each morning.

After the fire was going good and the chill was taken out of the room, he would come to the foot of the stairs and yell up the stairway for us boys to get up. Most of the time we were already awake from all the scraping of the grates and banging of the coal buckets, but the thought of getting out of that warm bed into a freezing room was enough to convince us we should stay put just a little longer. After a short period of grace and our father starting to put on coat and boots preparatory to going out to do the chores, he would again come to the foot of the stairs and yell more loudly and with more sternness in his voice that this time he wanted us to "get down here." This we knew was the last time he would call, and if there had to be a third time, he would probably come up with a switch. So, at the second yell, we'd jump out of bed, grab our clothes and race downstairs to get behind the dining room stove to put on our outer garments. We usually slept in our long-handled underwear and sometimes even left on our flannel shirts.

There were always a lot of chores to do every morning before we went to school or even before breakfast. There were pigs to feed, horses to be hayed and grained and cows to be milked. It was usually very dark when we started these chores, especially in the barn with the doors all closed. The only light we had was a smoky old kerosene lantern hanging high on a support beam in the middle of the barn. It was always quite a surprise to reach down into a dark barrel to get a scoop of feed and have a mouse run up your arm to get out of there.

When it came time to milk the cows, the lantern would be moved around into the cow section of the barn where the cows had been bedded down all night in their individual stanchions. Stanchions were a sort of vertical yoke, either made of wood or iron, which could be opened up to let the cow stick her head through to her feed box and then closed with a latch so she could not get her head out. During severe weather the cows

were kept in these stanchions all night. This was not a cruel thing to do because the stanchions were so constructed that the cow could lie down in her straw bed and chew her cud contentedly all night long.

Our milking operation was rather primitive by modern standards. We certainly did not have milking machines nor the electricity to run them. We had to sit down on a rickety old wooden stool on the right-hand side of the cow (she would kick you out of the stall if you started on the other side), set a bucket under her udder and start squeezing on her cold teats to get the milk flowing.

Since the cows had been lying in their stalls all night, their rear ends were quite messy from having to lie in their own excrement. Their tails were usually soaked with manure and urine, and whenever we would sit down to start milking, the cow from force of habit would switch her tail and fling her heavy-laden brush across our back or even sometimes give us a swipe in the face. If there happened to be manure on the udder, we would try to wipe it off with clean straw before starting to milk. Washing the udder as is done in present-day operations was out of the question in our barn in the winter. The water could have frozen on the udder and caused severe chapping which, in turn, would have caused the cow much pain in milking and a subsequent decrease in milk. After all, we did strain the milk through a fine mesh screen before we ran it through the separator and removed straw and most of the larger particulate matter.

Now before some of you city-bred readers begin to be turned off by such unsanitary handling of the milk, you should be told that the organisms which passed into the milk were normal soil organisms which were actually beneficial to digestion. If you are unconvinced by my statement, you need only read the label of your favorite yogurt and see the name of live organisms which had their origin in the cow barn. Actually the bacteria in milk are essential for normal souring, for making fine cheese and giving butter a distinctive flavor which is much preferred by some people. We were all very healthy in our family and didn't know that our method of handling milk was unsanitary.

Periodically our cows would give birth to a new calf and thus be stimulated to give more milk for the next several months. One such event I remember very well was when an old roan cow had her calf. I had heard my father say that we should keep an eye on Old Roan because she was about ready. Imagine my excitement when one evening I looked out into the back pasture and there was Old Roan with a beautiful, almost totally white baby calf staggering around her sides as newborn calves will do until they get their legs limbered up.

I was so excited about the new arrival that I didn't bother to inform my father or older brothers but raced out into the pasture with my little red wagon rattling along behind me. I did not realize at the time that animal mothers become very protective of their newborn and will often change their disposition radically toward their caretakers. I don't know if my

headlong dash toward the mother or the rattling wheels of my little wagon caused Old Roan to suddenly bellow and come charging toward me. I immediately did a quick turnaround and high-tailed it back to the barn with my little red wagon clattering along behind me. I would have soon become overtaken, but my brother Harold who was doing some chores in the barn heard all the commotion and quickly came to my rescue with a big stick. This caused the angry cow to turn and go back to her calf. I suspect the cow would have demolished the wagon first, but I'll never know.

Part of my daily duties around the barn was feeding the pigs. By pigs, I refer to all stages of a swine's age, sex and growth. Pigs are very prolific, having 10 to 12 babies at each farrowing, and their growth rate is phenomenal. A litter of 10 piglets can, if properly fed, weigh 200 pounds each, totalling a ton of pork in six months. Therefore, feeding the pigs was a very important chore. There was usually a drove of fattening pigs out in the hog lot east of the barn, and feeding them consisted of going out into the lot to a wagon load of ear corn and scooping out several bushels to the ground around the wagon.

Then there were separate pens each containing a sow with her baby pigs. These mothers were also very protective of their babies, and we learned very quickly to stay out of the shed where their babies were sleeping. I had an experience with a mother sow that did not have her pigs in the usual shed, but elected to go way out to the far end of the pasture and have her pigs in some tall weeds. My father missed seeing her one morning at feeding time so went looking for her. He found her out there in the weeds and knew when the sun became its hottest in the day, these little pigs would become badly sunburned. So he hitched a team of horses to the hay wagon and took it out to serve as a shade for the little pigs.

I was very curious to see the new litter that was born so far from home, so I slipped out there during the day to have a look. I knew that sows were often quite vicious if their babies were molested, so I crept up to the wagon very quietly and started peering through the weeds for a glimpse of the new arrivals. Suddenly the weeds exploded and out came the mother sow with a harsh roar and a full set of teeth glistening. She was every bit as intent on doing me in as would have been a Bengal tiger out of the jungle. I wasn't aware of my doing it, but I found myself up on that hay wagon out of reach of those jaws. And there I was treed for several minutes before the sow decided to go back to her babies and start nursing. I gave a giant leap off that wagon and lit out running and didn't look back until I was safely out of the pasture.

One of my least liked jobs was throwing down silage for the cows. We had a big tall silo at the north end of the barn that was as tall as the gable of the barn. We filled the silo each fall with chopped green corn and then fed it out daily during the winter months.

To get up into the silo one had to climb up on the outside on sort of an enclosed ladder. When there was the slightest wind blowing, this enclosure became a veritable wind tunnel, and while the so-called "wind chill index" had not yet been discovered, I was well aware of the effect of wind and cold every time I climbed that silo. My hands and feet were almost frozen by the time I got into the silo, and then I had to dig up that hard-packed (sometimes frozen) silage and throw it down the wind tunnel. The cows dearly loved this soured green corn, but my memories of it were not so pleasant.

Another climbing job that was not distasteful was getting up into the hayloft and throwing down hay for the horses. This was fun since it seemed warmer up there than down on the ground floor, and there was always the chance of catching a young pigeon while I was up there. Occasionally I would come upon an old stray tomcat that was also up there looking for a young pigeon. An occasional bunch of feathers would attest to his having done so. I greatly disliked these old semi-wild tomcats because if they ever found our old "mama" cat's kittens, they would kill them. So I would go at the old stray cat with upraised pitchfork and enjoy seeing him make a flying leap to the ground floor and disappear from the barn.

While on the subject of baby kittens, I should tell the story of my experience with a nest of kittens in that same hayloft. Our old bobtailed cat had apparently had another blessed event. I knew so because she had suddenly deflated her stomach. She was always very secretive about where she kept her new kittens, so it was always a challenge for me to find her new arrivals.

I had been watching her sneak out after her evening fill of warm skimmed milk, so decided to follow her and see where she went. First she slipped out to the wood pile in the chicken yard and snooped around there for a few minutes. Maybe she thought she would find a mouse for her kittens, but I suspect it was just a ruse to make me think her kittens were under there. After awhile she went around behind the hen house out of sight, but then I saw her go in a roundabout way through some weeds to the barn. I quickly ran down to the barn and peeked through a crack at the barn door just in time to see her disappear up the ladder into the hayloft. Now she was in my territory because I knew every nook and cranny in that loft, having played "hide and go seek" up there many times with neighboring kids. It didn't take me very long to find the mother and kittens in a secluded spot under a support brace covered with hay. The mother didn't seem at all surprised to see me, but lay quietly nursing her kittens and purring contentedly when I petted her. This was the most tranquilizing experience I think I had ever had.

The next thing I knew, I heard someone shout my name and looked up to see my father and a neighboring man in the dim light of a lantern. I had fallen asleep up there, and when I didn't show up at the house after dark, my father and the neighbor went looking for me. I was much embarrassed by this childish stunt and fully expected to get a licking for it. But my father apparently figured it was all done in innocence and gave me nothing more than a strong reprimand.

The feeding of livestock inside the barn in the wintertime was both convenient to the caretakers and humane to the animals. The only drawback to this method of handling was the accumulation of large quantities of manure and wet bedding. Every week or so we had to clean out the barn, and since we boys were in school every day during the week, this job naturally came on Saturday. And if we were going to have any free time on Saturday afternoon, we had to get out early and work like mad to get through by noon.

Cleaning out the barn was a backbreaking job. There would be large quantities of the manure and wet bedding, and it would be tightly packed because of the animals standing in it. We would hitch up a team of horses to the big wagon and pull the wagon alongside the barn as close to the barn door as possible. Then we would have to carry forksful of the manure to the barn door and throw it into the wagon. It might take us two or three hours to get the horse stable cleaned out; then there would be the cow barn to clean.

After we had a load of manure, we would drive to a field that was to be plowed the following spring and scatter the contents as widely and evenly as possible. Farming in those days was almost a closed system. We grew everything that was fed to our livestock, and all waste from those animals went back into the soil for the benefit of next year's crops.

You can imagine what we must have smelled like after a few hours of mucking around in a wagon load of manure, and it must have been pretty tough for our mother to set out dinner for us, but she never did complain because this was to be expected when working with livestock. Actually I suppose we smelled much the same way every evening when we came in from our chores at the barn, but after awhile no one seemed to notice.

Another cleaning job that had to be done, perhaps not so often, but detested just as much, was cleaning out the chicken house. Our mother maintained a flock of about 50 chickens, usually the Rhode Island Red breed which was the heavy, meatier breed and not particularly noted for their egg-laying ability. However, our mother took such good care of these old hens by carrying out warm drinking water in the winter and, of course, the tidbits from the kitchen by way of the slop bucket, so that this flock laid more eggs than they were genetically inclined to do. There not only were enough eggs for the table, but even a few left over to take to town for egg money. With this egg money, our mother was able to keep us in staples such as sugar and flour and even buy material for making an occasional dress for herself.

Back to cleaning out the hen house, the job never seemed to go away by just ignoring it, and our mother would keep after us until finally we had to comply. The work was not nearly as heavy as the barn cleaning, but it involved stooping and squatting along under the roosts to scrape out all the droppings the hens made while they were on the roosts at night. We usually bumped our heads or scraped our backs on the roosts and came out smelling just as badly as we did from the horse barn. But the job had to be done to keep the flock healthy.

Since there was not nearly as much of this as from the horse barn, we used a wheelbarrow to haul it out and spread on the garden. Chicken manure has a higher nitrate content than barnyard manure, so not as much was required for the garden.

Later on when young chicks were put out with their mothers in little houses, these too had to be cleaned regularly and even scrubbed with soapy water to keep down parasites.

This entire operation of raising baby chicks from eggs produced by the mature flock was fascinating to me. Every spring my mother would start saving what she called "setting" eggs. They were fertile eggs by reason of two or three old roosters being kept with the female flock. After she had what she considered enough for the summer operation, she'd place about 12 to 15 of these eggs under an old hen who had decided it was time for her to sit on some eggs. This was evidenced by her being found sitting on an empty nest at night when all the other hens had gone to roost. Usually there would be several of these

at this time of the year, but my mother would select only five or six to hatch the eggs she had saved for this purpose. The other sitters would be "thrown in jail to break them up." This meant they were put outside the hen house in a wire pen until they got over this urge to sit on a nest all day.

The "setting" hens that were selected were placed in nesting boxes in a separate little room at one side of the chicken house and were fed and watered separately from the main flock. So dedicated were these old hens that they had to be lifted off their nests each time they were fed and watered. My mother would never allow anyone other than herself to tend these old hens. Any strange person or unusual handling might "break them up" (cause them to lose their brooding instinct). This would be a catastrophe because a whole clutch of eggs would be lost.

After 21 days of this brooding operation, the eggs would hatch on schedule, and the mother hen and baby chicks would have to be moved outside to individual coops. These were little shed-like structures that had hinged doors that could be closed at night to lock the mother and chicks inside to protect them from predators such as skunks, weasels, rats and even old stray tomcats.

For the first few days the old hen had to be tied to the coop to give her and the chicks a sense of belonging to this particular house. This was to keep her from wandering away or crowding her chicks in another coop with another family.

These coops had removable wooden floors, and every week the coops had to be upended and the floor scraped free of droppings and scrubbed with hot sudsy water as mentioned earlier. This little job was usually held over until Saturday morning when we boys would much rather have been fishing or off tramping around in the woods, but it had to be done. After a few days the old hen would be released from the cord that kept her tied to the coop, and she could take her chicks out around the chicken yard and teach them how to scratch for bugs and earthworms. But each night they would faithfully return to the same coop to spend the night. One of our chores was to go out after it began to get dark and lock the doors of all the coops.

In about three or four weeks the chicks had grown into long-legged juveniles and were ready to make it on their own. The mother hen could no longer accommodate them under her wings at night, so she was put back into the hen house, but the chicks continued to sleep in their coops at night.

It soon became evident which chicks were to become roosters and which would become hens. Usually it was about half and half. Since there was no need for more than three or four roosters as replacements in the mature flock, the largest of the males would be sacrificed for Sunday dinners or even during the week when company came. By the end of the growing season when it came time to put the summer's hatch into the chicken house, the rooster population would be down to the three or four necessary for next year's production.

Getting back to chores, each spring our father would plow the garden and an outlying plot for growing potatoes. The garden area had to be worked down with hand tools because there was a fence around it, and horse-drawn disks and harrows could not be maneuvered around in such a small enclosure. Garden tillers powered by gasoline engines had not even been dreamed of in those days. The planting of the garden was usually done by our mother because she knew from years of experience just how deep to plant and how far apart the seeds should be sown.

The potato patch was our father's province. The patch was usually located out in an open area where horse-drawn implements could be used to work the ground. He even used a walking plow to lay out the rows, then drop the potato seed down the furrow in measured spacing. A horse-drawn harrow was used to cover the seed and level off the patch.

After all the planting was done, child labor was brought into the business of keeping the weeds out of the garden and potato patch. This labor started just about the time school was out for the summer when we boys thought we were free for fishing, swimming and other important activities. It also coincided with hot weather — the hotter the weather, the faster the weeds grew. And, of course, there were numerous other jobs around the farm waiting for us, such as plowing corn, making hay and harvesting grain. Our dream of summer freedom was just a dream.

Chapter III

Weekends and Rainy Days

TO MOST CHILDREN IN MODERN SOCIETY, after a week in school, the weekend means two days of freedom to do just about anything they please. But, "when I was a kid" (there's that title again) things were different. Saturday was a time to catch up on all those odd jobs described in the previous chapter. Fortunately many of them were seasonal jobs and didn't come every Saturday, but there was usually something that had to be done to help keep things going on the farm. At the time, I thought it was very unfair, and I'm sure I did a lot of fussing about the work, but after several years of reflection I realized we were not permanently scarred and probably benefited from the responsibility it engendered within us. Actually our father seldom required us to work all day on Saturday, but would assign us a task and suggest that if we got done by noon, we could be free that afternoon. This enticement usually spurred us to work twice as hard and thus do a whole day's work in half the time.

Sunday was a different matter. Because of the religious beliefs of our parents, there was to be no work except the necessary chores of feeding and caring for livestock. Of course, with our mother it was almost like "business as usual." She had to race around early in the morning before church tending her chickens and getting ready for a big meal for after church. More than likely, an entire family would be invited to our house for Sunday dinner, and extra quantities had to be planned for that likelihood.

It seemed to me this guest business was never planned

ahead, but determined after church when everyone was visiting and inviting each other to come to dinner. Occasionally we would get to go to someone else's house for dinner, and all that food our mother had gotten ready had to be held over into the following week. But more often than not, our mother won out, or should I say "lost out" on this bidding for dinner guests. She was the one who had to hurry home and prepare a big meal for company. Too many of the other good housewives could come up with some excuse for not being able to host the dinner this time.

There were very few times we ever missed going to both Sunday School and church. Even when it was raining and mud was ankle deep (there were no hard surface roads), we would hitch up a team of horses to the big wagon or the surrey and go. Part of this punctuality was, of course, because our father either had to preach the sermon or to sit on the pulpit while a visiting preacher spoke. His presence was expected, and proper decorum of his children was expected. Sometimes the latter was not always adhered to. One of my favorite stunts to while away the time while my father was preaching was catching flies. We had no screens on the big windows of the church, and during the warmer months when the windows were open there were lots of flies attracted to the odors of the congregation. I became quite proficient with my right hand in making a quick sweep at a sitting fly and squashing him in my fingers. I made no noise in this activity, but am sure the entire row of listeners were keeping an eye on me to see if I scored.

Another breach of decorum that I have been very much ashamed of most of my life occurred one night at communion. Our church had a ritual of handing along a strip of unleavened bread and each person turning to his neighbor, break off a small piece and very solemnly speak a little verse about this being the "body of Christ." I was sitting next to a boy about my age who perhaps was not properly indoctrinated into our church dogma who did not know the verse. After some hesitation, he leaned over to me and very solemnly said, "Have a cracker." Somehow this struck me as being very funny, and I let out a snort that attracted everyone's attention and then had to hold my hands over my mouth to keep from exploding in laughter. I never did know what happened to that piece of baked dough, but somehow the ritual continued. I fully expected a whipping from my father after services were over, but somehow he sensed my remorse and said nothing about the matter.

I spoke of our regularity in going to church, but there were rare occasions when the elements were so severe as to make our attendance foolhardy. It was one of those days when there had been a heavy snow the night before and the morning turned out clear but bitter cold. It must have been several degrees below zero, and our parents decided this was one of the times we should not go to church. Big brother Harold said this weather wouldn't keep him from going, he would just walk to church. Then second brother Del decided he could walk to church also. I'm sure neither of them wanted to do this because of strong religious convictions, but rather an inherent determination to prove themselves capable of withstanding the challenge. Del didn't have a cap with ear flaps and steadfastly refused to wear a stocking cap, which exposed his ears to the bitter cold.

I wasn't there to see it, but Harold and several other folks told us afterward that when Del got to church and started warming himself over the floor furnace, his ears began to swell and got all out of proportion to the rest of his face. He had frozen his ears on the way to church, and when they thawed out the inflammatory reaction caused the swelling. I'm sure his ears must have hurt considerably, but he wouldn't admit to any problem when he got home.

Sunday afternoons were supposed to reflect the true meaning of a "day of rest." We kids were allowed to go out and play, but we were to do nothing that was productive such as going fishing in the summertime or rabbit hunting in the winter. We were supposed to stay at home and relax. That was out of the question for a couple of young boys. As soon as Sunday dinner was over, Del and I would go outside to play. Most of our play consisted of seeing who could run the fastest, throw a rock the farthest or chin ourselves the most times. Since Del was two years older than I, there wasn't much question of who won. But I never hesitated to try. Sometimes this determination to keep up with Del got me into some perilous situations, such as the time we climbed up on the roof of the house. Another time Del climbed to the top of the windmill and dared me to climb as high. I got almost to the top but made the mistake of looking down. I literally froze to the steel ladder and was afraid to come back down. Finally after some contemplation I managed to make the first step down and finally the rest of the way. I never tried that stunt again.

Then there was the dare to crawl across the big opening to the hayloft of the barn. Our barn was a big, high barn with a wide opening in the gable of one end where hay was hoisted in by use of ropes and pulleys. This opening was about 15 feet from the ground, and to a small boy that looked like at least 40 feet. There was a 2 x 6 board across the base of the opening to which the hay door was hinged. The door was left open during most of the summer when hay was being made to fill the loft for winter. It was this opening which Del dared me to crawl across. He had already made his crossing and was "egging" me on to do likewise. I got about halfway across before I "froze" and couldn't move. Fortunately the hay was piled up inside far enough to cushion my fall, so I pushed myself off the narrow ledge to the hay inside. I was so terrified of that climb that I had nightmares of falling out of that hay barn doorway until I was fully grown.

I wouldn't say that all our play was of such a dangerous nature, but somehow I always seemed to end up with the "short end of the stick." Often our so-called play took on a more aggressive nature. I guess modern psychologists would call it sibling rivalry, but we called it fighting. Again, two years difference in our ages put me at considerable disadvantage and earned me the name of Cry Baby.

One of our Sunday afternoon games was called corn cob fighting. This took place in the barn, usually on a rainy afternoon when we couldn't get outside. There were no particular rules to this game, just an unwritten agreement to not start fighting until each participant had a goodly number of corn cobs accumulated as ammunition. The battlefield was across the hay mangers which separated the horse stalls from the feeding room. Naturally there were no horses in the barn at the time of battle. At the mutually agreed word "Go," we would start throwing corn cobs at each other over the manger. If the going got too hot for one of the combatants, he would duck down behind the manger and gather up more cobs for a fresh assault. Occasionally someone would get lucky and catch his opponent stooped over to pick up more cobs and he could "whang" him on the rear where the pants were stretched tight. The injured one would jump up quickly in retaliation and say, "That didn't hurt," but if one dared peek over the manger after such a direct hit, he might see his opponent rubbing the injured part.

After the battle had gone on for some time and both parties were nearly out of cobs, a secret weapon might be brought into play. It was a big old fat cob that had been soaking in manure and urine for several weeks, and it was heavy enough to do bodily harm if it connected. The battle was over when someone, usually me, got whacked up beside the face with such a cob and the injured one had to go to the house to clean up.

I can't remember whether this next episode came on a rainy Saturday afternoon or on Sunday afternoon. Del and I were at loose ends and couldn't find anything to do. My old bobtailed cat and I had discovered earlier that there were some mice in a stack of sheaf oats in one corner of the hayloft. The mice had been in there for some time and had multiplied mightily. When I showed Del how the mice would run out when a sheaf of oats was picked up, he quickly came up with an idea of capturing these mice and creating a menagerie. We each got an old pair of leather gloves so we could catch the mice without being bitten. Since the sheaf oats were in a section of the loft directly above the cow shed, we set an old cream can on the floor of the cow shed exactly beneath a knothole in the floor of the loft. Then we started our mouse-catching operation. It was great fun grabbing the mice as they ran for cover when we moved another sheaf of oats. When we had a mouse in each hand, we would poke them through the knothole and watch them fall into the cream can below. After we had moved the bundles of oats several times and exhausted the supply of mice, we went down to the cow shed to view our catch. It was the wildest sight I had ever seen. We must have had 50 mice in that can, squeaking and scrambling all over one another.

The next step was to find something to keep them in for pets. We finally found an old wooden box which, after some modification, was considered suitable. A partition in the box provided for an upstairs and downstairs with a little notched stick for a stairway. We even provided a little swing in one section in case the mice might want to play. The entire front was covered with screen wire so we could see everything that was going on.

Now we were ready to show off our accomplishment. We raced up to the house and into the kitchen with our menagerie and proudly displayed our prize possession. Our mother was usually pretty cool-headed when it came to dealing with mice and small snakes, but this exhibition was too much for her. She screamed at us to get those nasty things out of her kitchen and take them down to the pond and drown them. Her direct orders were sustained by our father, and the mice had to go.

My interest in mice continued in spite of this setback, and I later built a little wheel cage into which I could place a captured mouse and watch him turn the wheel as he ran to get away. We always seemed to have lots of mice on our farm, and

I suppose it was natural for me to try to find a use for them. My most popular mouse item was a mouse puppet. I followed my big brother Harold's technique of skinning an animal and stretching the hide on a board until it dried. This was a bit tedious on a mouse, but after a little practice it got easier. After the mouse skin was dry, I could stick it on my thumb and wiggle it to scare the girls at school. All the boys at school wanted one, but I think the teacher put the quietus on my enterprise.

Getting back to free time on Saturday afternoons during the school months, I think our father nearly always let us have that time off even though there might still be work to be done. In the wintertime I could hardly wait to get out in any kind of weather, preferably with snow on the ground, to hunt for rabbits. I had learned to do this at a very early age by tagging along after my big brother Harold. He was quite an accomplished hunter and trapper, spending much of his free time in the woods or along brushy ditches hunting for rabbits or setting traps for skunks, possums, raccoons or any kind of wildlife prevalent in the area. I would tag along while he was setting his traps and usually got up very early the next morning to get to the traps before he did.

One such incident which I shall not forget was when he had set out a new kind of box trap down in the woods about a quarter of a mile from our house. The trap was a simple box with one end open and fitted with a swinging door made of heavy wire. The door was designed to swing in when pushed by the animal but would not swing out to allow the animal to escape. I had seen Harold set the trap and bait it with a piece of apple. I think he hoped to catch a possum or maybe even a coon.

It came a big snow that night, and Harold decided he wasn't going to look at the trap right away. But that didn't deter me. I bundled up and took off in snow that was up to my knees in some spots. When I got near the trap, I could see something was in it. I raced over and looked in. If it had been a skunk, he would have hit me right in the face with his repellant, but it was a rabbit.

I quickly reached in and grabbed the rabbit by the hind legs, pulled it out of the box and very excitedly took off running back to the house. On the way I had to go around a corner post that was held in place by a guy wire made of twisted barbed wire. I didn't see the guy wire because the snow had covered it. I went plunging around the corner post and got one leg under the guy wire. When I jerked loose, I felt a stinging in my leg but was so excited and perhaps numb with cold that I didn't bother to see what happened. When I got home and showed the rabbit, still very much alive and kicking, my mother saw my pants leg was soaked with blood and quickly stripped me down and found an ugly bleeding gash in my leg from the barbs on the guy wire. It wasn't until I saw the wound that I realized I was hurt and started crying.

Another incident of my looking at one of Harold's traps, and one I would like to forget, was the time I sneaked out before daylight to look at a trap he had set under a big cement bridge along the road about a quarter of a mile east of our house. It was a steel trap, and Harold had set it in the ditch under the bridge and baited with part of an old dead hen. I knew the trap was there and just couldn't wait until daylight to see what might be caught.

I slipped out of the house while my father and two older brothers were at the barn doing the chores. I raced down the road to the big cement bridge. It really wasn't a very big bridge, but to a very small boy it seemed like a long way down to the bottom of the ditch. I peered over the edge and searched the gloom for any sign of an animal. Suddenly I saw something white moving around in the spot where I knew the trap to be. I strained my eyes as hard as I could to try to make out what it was. Then it popped into my head that this was a broad-striped skunk with only the white stripe showing in the dark. I wasn't about to go down there for a closer look but ran as fast as I could to report the catch to Harold.

Harold hadn't planned to go look at the trap that morning because it might make him late for school. But after hearing my excited report, he made the trip to the bridge to see what was caught. When he returned, he very disgustedly told me there wasn't a thing in that trap, it hadn't even been thrown. I couldn't believe it. I just knew I had seen a broad-striped skunk down there, and that evening after school I made a trip to see for sure. I even got down in the ditch, to find the trap nor the bait had been disturbed. It was very embarrassing to me and, of course, my brothers wouldn't let me forget that I had made it all up from pure imagination. It wasn't until years later that I conceived the idea that there really was a skunk down there snooping around but was too smart to be caught.

In the summertime when there was no school and we were not required to be helping with raising crops or harvesting, we would seize on every opportunity to go fishing along the Wakenda Creek. This was a very small, tree-lined creek about a mile north of our house, and whenever we finished hoeing weeds in the garden, cutting jimson weeds in the barn lot or replanting corn or any of the hundreds of jobs we seemed to have, we would dig a few fishing worms, get our fish hooks and lines and head for the Wakenda. Our fishing equipment was rather primitive — an old cork out of a jug or even just a half of a corn cob for a float with several feet of stout string wrapped around it. We would have several hooks stuck in a separate cork in case we lost a hook or so in some brush in the water. We seldom carried a fishing pole to the creek because there were plenty of willows and maples growing along the creek bank which could be cut for that purpose. Our bait was

kept in a flat Prince Albert tobacco can
that we could carry in our hip pocket. The
corks with the fishing lines wrapped around
them could be carried in the front pockets of
our bib overalls, thus leaving our hands free

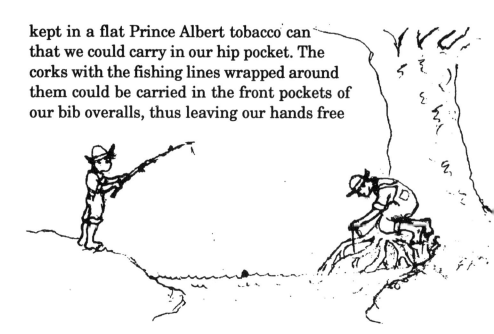

for throwing rocks, making a whistle with a blade of grass or
scattering milkweed seed into the wind.

Usually the creek was a shallow stream that could be waded
barefoot by rolling up our pants to our knees, but there were
occasional deeper holes where catfish or sun perch were hiding out. Our favorite fishing spot was in a rather deep hole
under the roots of a giant maple tree. The water at flood time
had washed out the soil from under part of the roots so that
we could crawl out on the roots and dangle a baited hook down
between the roots to the dark pool beneath. There was almost
always an instant bite on our line under these roots, but getting the fish out was a different matter. The fish or the hook
would hang up on a root, and we would end up losing the fish
and the hook. When we began to run short of hooks, we would
start fishing out in the open with a pole. We seldom ever caught
anything larger than our hand, but we faithfully carried all
except the very tiniest home for our mother to cook.

If we weren't catching any fish or had run out of bait or
hooks, we would spend the rest of the afternoon wading up or
down the creek trying to catch frogs or crawfish. One day we
discovered frogs were hiding in crawfish holes in the creek bed

just above the water level. We started reaching in those holes and pulling out frogs. I reached into an especially large hole and got my fingers around what I thought was a frog. When I pulled it out where I could see, it was a coil of a big black-snake. Needless to say, we quit sticking our hands in any more crawfish holes.

We never carried any drinking water with us to the creek because downstream from our favorite fishing hole was a spring running out of the bank of the creek. We always visited that spring on our fishing trips. One very hot and dry summer day we went to the spring for a drink and found it had dried up. We were very thirsty so went back up the creek looking for another source of water. Suddenly we realized we were walking in trickling clear, cool water. Why not just have a drink out of the stream.

We quickly got down and drank our fill and thought it very good water. We got up and continued on upstream. Just around a bend in the creek we found, much to our dismay, an old dead sow lying in the water. She was very badly bloated and was discharging fluids from body openings into the stream of water from which we had just had our fill. We never told our parents about this experience but spent several anxious days wondering if we were going to come down with the same disease that killed the old sow.

I said the creek was usually a very shallow stream that could be waded, but there were times in the spring of the year after very heavy rains when the little creek became a raging torrent. It even sometimes got out of its banks and flooded the low lands on either side. One such time we had heard the creek was higher than ever, and Del and I just had to see it. We took off barefooted because we wanted to wade in the flood water. Of course, we didn't tell our parents we were going to do that.

When we got in sight of the creek, sure enough it met all expectations. There was water all over the flat land on either side of the creek, and all that could be seen to mark the location of the creek itself were some trees standing above the water along the banks, and the old concrete bridge built high above the creek bed to prevent it from being washed away by just such floods as this.

Del and I immediately decided we were going to follow the road that was under water and wade out to the bridge to see what the creek looked like. The water was not very swift over the roadway nor was it very deep. We easily rolled up our britches legs and waded out until we came to the approaches of the bridge. The water was much swifter here, but we felt very confident by having come this far, and the bridge looked like a safe haven. Soon we were standing on the bridge, high and dry.

The creek itself was really a wild thing, swirling and roaring through the bridge abutments and barely able to pass under the floor of the bridge. After watching this spectacle for several minutes, we began looking for some further challenge. It must have been Del, because I would have never dreamed of jumping off into that raging torrent. We both thought we were good swimmers because we had learned to swim in our new big pond our father had recently built, but this was something else. It soon became a dare, and neither of us could admit to being afraid.

We were soon stripped of our clothes and out over the railing. At the word "go," we plunged into the swirling water. The realization that we had made a mistake came very quickly. The water came at us in swirls, churning us around and propelling us downstream at a frightening rate. Downstream was a big tree swaying in the water. Part of its roots had been undermined, and it had fallen over into the current and was half submerged. By the time we had gone this far, we were ready to grab at anything to halt our wild rush downstream. We both grabbed at the bobbing limbs and hung on. Suddenly the pull of the water against our bodies caused the tree limb to fully submerge, taking us down with it. That was when real panic set in for me. I turned loose of that tree limb and fought back up to the surface coughing and sputtering and all of the time being carried rapidly downstream. I looked for Del, and there he was right alongside of me. Fortunately there was a curve in the creek, and as we were swept close to the bank, we reached out and grabbed some bushes and pulled ourselves out into the shallow water on the bank. We waded back to the bridge, put on our clothes and went home. Naturally, we didn't tell our parents what we had done.

As we grew older, our trips to the Wakenda Creek became less frequent. Del had discovered the world of books and spent most of his free time reading everything he could get his hands on. He had soon read all the books in the school library and would borrow novels from older boys in the community.

Since the reading matter Del liked didn't yet appeal to me, I started looking for entertainment and companionship with neighboring kids and with my nephew, Gwendle, who was just a few years younger than I. The good times we had together would fill many more pages and would best be described in another manuscript.

Chapter IV

School Days

SINCE A VERY HIGH PERCENTAGE of my time as a kid was spent in school, I would be remiss if I did not relate some of those experiences. I did not particularly enjoy school because I was a slow learner, and my memories of events pertaining to the learning process were not especially happy ones. Perhaps that accounts for this chapter of my childhood being delayed to this late point in the narrative.

Since my parents chose to live in this distinctly rural, almost backwoods neighborhood, the school I attended was primitive by any modern standards. It was a long one-room wooden structure with tall windows on both sides. There was a porch across the front supported by steel pipes which were suitable for small fry making like whirligigs by grasping the pipe by both hands and pushing the body around with the feet. On frosty mornings these pipes served as a learning process,

wherein the older boys of the school would dare the little kids to stick their tongue out and touch the very cold pipe. The result was an instant freezing of their tongue to the pipe, and if they jerked away immediately, they would leave the outer portion of their tongue on the pipe. However, if they would wait just a few seconds, the warmth of their tongue would melt the icy contact and allow them to go free with an intact tongue. This was a learning experience that most of us went through and never forgot.

Our school had a big bell housed in a cupola-like structure known as a belfry, all of which was perched on top of the ridge of the roof at the front end of the school. A rope extended down through the ceiling of the school room which, when pulled vigorously, would cause the bell to ring very loudly, presumably to wake up all kids in the neighborhood who forgot to go to school that day. It was also used to signal the end of recess, a 15-minute playtime at mid-morning and mid-afternoon, and for the close of the noon hour. Occasionally the teacher's pet might be allowed to ring the bell.

The desks were arranged in rows from front to back, or perhaps I should say from back to front. The teacher's desk sat at the opposite end of the front entrance, and once inside of the school the front was considered where the teacher sat. This was always a little confusing to me, but it worked out pretty well because late comers could sneak in the door, and if the teacher's back was turned, they might slip to their desk unnoticed. However, the teacher nearly always caught them, which led us to believe she had eyes in the back of her head.

Most of our teachers were barely out of adolescence themselves, having just recently graduated from high school and a short course in teaching at a teacher's college, but to us little country kids they represented authority and knowledge beyond belief. Only in our higher grades did we begin to suspect some of those teachers didn't know much about scientific matters.

There was a rather high rate of turnover among these teachers. Either they found the profession to be somewhat less than expected or the boyfriend back home would want to get married, and they surely didn't want to pass up that opportunity. One year when I was in about the third grade we had four different teachers. Naturally our learning had to suffer from that many interruptions.

As I said, I was a slow learner, particularly in arithmetic. I think I was in the seventh grade before I finally mastered the multiplication tables, and when we got to the place in the arithmetic book where we had to solve those riddle-like problems like how many apples Jack would have if he gave Jane three apples of the original 10 he had but had eaten two on the way to school. That second consideration of thinking about Jack eating those apples on the way to school would completely throw my thinking off the track.

I tried taking my problems home to get help from my father, but that was a mistake. He was very proficient in mathematics and was noted for his ability to figure how many tons of hay in a stack or bushels of corn in a round pen. Most all the neighbors in the community would come to him to figure these problems for them. But my little problems with apples were so elementary, he couldn't understand why I couldn't figure them out myself, and after awhile became so exasperated with me that he called me a "dummy." After that, all I could think about was how dumb I was. I'm sure my father didn't intend to hurt my feelings because he was very gentle with me in other ways, but I carried the scar of that humiliation for many years.

Our little one-room school had very few of the niceties of modern schools. The toilets were typical country two-holers located at opposite corners of the schoolyard. The only running water in these was what we contributed and, as with the privy at home, a trip to one of these through a blinding snowstorm was pretty rough. In order to use the toilet we had to wave our hand to attract the attention of the teacher and ask to "leave the room." Everyone knew what that meant, and there was usually a bit of snickering.

About the only other time we were allowed to leave our seats other than for recitation was to sharpen our pencil. We didn't have a pencil sharpener, but nearly every boy carried a pocket knife. There was a coal bucket behind the furnace where we could go to sharpen our pencil and put the shavings in the bucket. One of the most frequent visitors to the coal bucket was a big overgrown perennial student who couldn't seem to pass the grades and was almost a full-grown man before he was finally released from school. Bud, which was his name, didn't really need to sharpen his pencil, but when he was up there behind the furnace, he couldn't be seen by the teacher but could be seen by the bulk of the student body. This gave him an opportunity to start making monkey faces at the kids. This wasn't difficult for Bud because he was sort of a "throw-back" to begin with, and his simian antics soon brought titterings from the students. It was then that the teacher would realize Bud was still there and call out, "Bu-ud," and Bud would answer "Maa-amm," and the teacher would tell him to take his seat. Bud seldom went to his seat the first time this little dialogue was performed but would remain very quietly for a few minutes to see if the teacher might forget he was there. This exchange might have to be repeated two or three times before Bud would finally slouch off to his seat. The young teacher was not about to come around the stove and confront Bud because apparently there was a bit of fear of this big, un-gainly man-boy who was probably near the same age as the teacher and twice as big.

The desks in our schoolroom were arranged in three rows with a narrow passageway along each side of the room and a wider passageway on either side of the center row of desks. These passageways permitted any student in the room to leave his seat and pass to the front of the room whenever his grade was called for recitation. This immediately points out that every class from first grade through the eighth had to recite their lessons before the entire school. It was sort of a built-in entertainment for all the students listening in. But before you conclude that this must have been a terrible system of teaching, it actually turned out to be quite advantageous as a learning tool. By the time a student had reached the third or fourth grade, he had been exposed to all the material being taught at least twice, and if he were highly observant, he would have absorbed most of what was being taught through all eight grades. My brother Del was allowed to completely skip one grade because he knew all the material being taught. He went on to high school and led his class in grade points, apparently not suffering from this early method of teaching.

I did not get to skip any classes because as soon as the State Board of Education got wind of what was being done, they promptly put a stop to such unorthodox methods of promotion.

Our house was approximately three-fourths of a mile from the schoolhouse, and the greater part of that distance was over a muddy, seldom-used lane, almost completely overgrown by brush and trees. During rainy weather or snowstorms this back road was very difficult to negotiate by foot, either because of the tenacious clay that would stick to our overshoes or snowdrifts that sometimes were up to our hips.

When I first started to school, I had the opportunity of riding in a buggy with a neighbor and his son who lived almost a mile farther than we did. The father was a cantankerous old fellow who didn't have much use for schooling but was forced by law to see his son through grade school. My brother Del usually disdained riding in the buggy with us, partially because of the crowding and particularly because he disliked the somewhat prejudiced views of the old man.

There was one time, however, when Del consented to get into the buggy with us. It was pouring down rain, and Del was slogging along the muddy road getting soaking wet when we came along. The old man felt sorry for Del and let him in, mud and all. On the way Del started complaining about having to recite a poem for the Literary Hour at the close of school. Apparently he felt that reciting a poem was sissy stuff, and he was about to rebel at doing it. The old fellow driving us to school saw his chance to strike a blow at the establishment, so he told Del he would give him a poem to recite and proceeded to do so. Later that afternoon when classes were through recitations, it came time for the Literary Hour. Readings were given and poems were recited. When Del's time came, this is what he recited:

"I had a little pony, I fed him on hay,
He heisted up his tail and blew it all away."

Needless to say, the poem was a big hit with the students but not funny to the teacher.

There were other after-school performances which contributed to the overall education of the pupils such as ciphering matches and spelling bees. We didn't have such things as football or basketball practice. We didn't know what a football looked like and didn't have a basketball until I was almost ready to graduate.

The ciphering matches were contests in simple arithmetic in the lower grades, working up to more complicated square root in the upper grades. The system was to send two pupils of equal grade level to the blackboard, and the teacher would give out a set of figures for addition or subtraction. We had one girl in our class who could add faster than any of the rest of us by pecking her chalk on the board at a very rapid rate. She would peck and count so fast and noisily that it sounded like a woodpecker on a tin roof. I think the noise so flustered her competitor that she nearly always won. After she had ciphered down everyone in our class, she would still be at the board for the next higher grade. But here she might be matched against someone who had learned to calculate across the column of figures as they were being given. I never did know how that worked, but somehow the contestant could quickly calculate the answer and write it down almost immediately after the figures were read by the teacher.

As I said before, I was a "dummy" when it came to figures, and I was usually knocked out of contention the first time up, but spelling was something else. For some reason my mind could visualize the spelling of a word after I had seen it only a time or two. For the spelling contest, the teacher would pick two of the upperclassmen and have them choose up sides. They would, of course, try to choose the best spellers first as they worked their way down through the grades. After all pupils had been chosen, there would be a long row of pupils standing along the wall on either side of the room. The teacher would begin by giving out little simple words to the first and second graders, and when anyone missed a word they had to take their seat. As the words became progressively more difficult, there would be only a few still standing to battle it out for top speller. I was usually fortunate enough to be among the final few.

During the school day when we were not reciting, we were supposed to be at our desks studying for our next recitation. Very few of us did so. If we were not listening to the recitation of another class at the front of the room, we would be doing what we liked to do best so long as we stayed in our seat and didn't make noise. Some of the little girls would cut out paper dolls, and the older ones would peek at the boys and giggle. The younger boys would carve their initials in the wooden desk and rub spit in it to make it look as if some former pupil had done it.

My specialty was drawing pictures of farm animals. I had learned to do this at a very tender age when Del and I would be cooped up in the house on a stormy Sunday afternoon. We would start quarreling, and to make us behave our mother would suggest we see who could draw the best picture. She would get an old piece of brown wrapping paper, cut it in two pieces and put us in opposite ends of the room to make our drawings. It was usually a picture of some farm animal since we had never seen a lion or tiger or elephant, although we occasionally tried. After we had drawn our picture, we would take it around for the family to judge who had drawn the best one. Most of the time Del's picture was judged best because he was more experienced than I, but sometimes we'd spend most of an afternoon at this, sprawled out on the floor of the kitchen or living room.

It was this experience I used when drawing pictures at school to be admired by my schoolmates. One teacher even called on me to help out with a problem child. A little boy first-grader was so frightened of school and homesick that he would cry almost all day long, not loudly but a sniffling that drove the teacher up the wall. The other kids called him "windsucker," which didn't help his problem at all. One day the teacher realized he had quit sniffling and found him absorbed with my drawing a picture of a horse. Thereafter when the boy started his uncontrollable sobbing, she would call on me to draw him another horse. Eventually he came to enjoy school because he was making a scrapbook of horses I was drawing for him.

Recess was a big occasion for all. I'm sure even the teacher enjoyed a little respite from trying to teach and maintain order in a whole roomful of squirming kids. There was no organized play at our school, although there were certain games we played that had rather loosely applied rules. One game that could be played by the entire student body was called "Black Man." I don't know how the game originated or how it got its name, but I don't think there were any ethnic connotations. At least we never gave them any thought. The game was played by all students lining up on either side of a large open area. Two or more of the older children were selected to be "it" and were allowed to roam freely in the open area. At a signal everyone on the two sides were supposed to run to the opposite side. The "its" would try to tag as many runners as possible, and once a runner was tagged he had to go to the sidelines and be content with cheering on his buddies. Very quickly the game would end with two or three very fleet runners trying to dodge the equally fleet "its." When all were finally tagged, the game would be repeated. This was not a very complicated game but gave everyone an opportunity to whoop and holler and let off steam from the confinement of the classroom.

A somewhat similar game known as "knock the buck" was sometimes played mostly by older boys, wherein a three-legged stick called the buck was set up in the middle of the court by a buck tender, while the rest of the participants, each wielding a big stick or club, would line up on either side of the arena. As soon as the buck tender placed the three-legged stick in an upright position, everyone on the sidelines was permitted to throw his club at the buck and try to knock it over. If the buck was successfully knocked over, everyone could run out to get their club while the buck tender was having to set the buck back up. But if the buck tender could get the buck set back up and catch someone in the act of picking up their club, then that person had to be the buck tender.

As one could readily see, this game was a pretty dangerous proposition for the buck tender and was usually ended by one of the little kids having to be buck tender and getting hit by one of the many flying clubs, after which he would run bawling to the teacher. The teacher would come out and stop the game by either breaking the legs off the buck or burning it in the furnace. The game couldn't be played again until someone could come up with another three-legged stick cut from the crotch of a young tree.

Various other games could be played, mostly by girls who did not wish to play such rough games. These consisted of hopscotch, fox and goose in season, upset the fruit basket in the schoolhouse during stormy weather and a wide variety of other sissy games. Little boys could play stick horse, a game wherein each boy would climb astride a long stick and prance around the playground pretending he had a very spirited steed. Tiring of that, they might try acting as if they were driving an automobile. This consisted of grasping a short stick by each end and racing about the playground steering the stick so as to simulate hairpin curves and very steep hills. Since Model T

Fords were the only motor vehicles known to most of us at the time, we had to make a sputtering sound with our lips to sound similar to the Model T. This was accomplished by fluttering the lips, along with considerable spit being sprayed about and occasionally running down on the chin.

There were, of course, many other games such as string ball and shinny, which could be played when the weather was cooperative. Our playground was just a dirt courtyard that had to be chopped free of weeds each September when school started. The second day of school each boy was asked to bring a hoe or shovel with which to clean off the playground. This was usually accomplished in short order, frequently before the bell rang on the second day. Each boy was anxious to show off his strength and ability at the beginning of the school term just to demonstrate how much he had grown during the summer. But naturally, when it rained, our playground became a sloppy mess and impossible for any of our outside games.

During such rainy days the older boys of the school would not stoop to staying in the schoolhouse during the noon hour and play girl games, but instead would congregate in the horse shed. This building was off to one side of the schoolyard and consisted of two stalls for tying horses in case anyone rode to school. However, the stalls were seldom used. Even the teacher walked to school since she boarded with a family living very close to the schoolhouse. There were usually only about seven or eight boys in the school who were old enough or worldly enough to withstand some of the rough and sometimes risque activities that went on in the horse shed. Younger boys that might have a tendency to cry and run tell the teacher what was going on were usually very quickly discouraged from staying, by a little pinching or head-thumping.

After all the cry babies were safely in the schoolhouse, the remaining "toughies" would haul out their smoking equipment, which usually consisted of pieces of dried grapevine or ground-up mullen leaves, a weed also known as Indian tobacco. Only one boy was allowed to smoke at any one time because if more than one were to light up, the smoke might start creeping out under the eaves of the shed and alert the teacher that something was going on. Each boy would take his turn and try to outdo the others by trying to make smoke rings or inhale without coughing.

When we ran out of smoking material or matches, we would usually start showing off our physical skills, such as chinning ourselves or standing on our head, which was sort of a messy thing to do in a horse stable. Each activity was repeated by each boy until the best was determined by acclamation.

One such competitive activity that stood out in my mind was a mock boxing match in which I was a participant. None of us local boys had ever witnessed a boxing match or even engaged in a fist fight. To have been caught doing so by our parents would have resulted in a good whipping. But a new family had moved into our neighborhood, and two boys about my age had started to our school. The older boy was a friendly sort and well-liked by most all of us, but the younger one was a boisterous, rough-and-tumble sort who was given to bullying younger children. I disliked him very much and would have very little to do with him. He may have construed that to mean I was a little bit afraid of him, because one day when we were lolling around in the horse shed with nothing in particular to do, he started showing what a good shadow boxer he was and danced over to me and asked if I would like him to show me what an uppercut was. I suggested he could show me on himself. But he kept jumping around in front of me and suddenly swung a low looping left fist which was supposed to just barely miss my chin, but he miscalculated and caught me on the chin with a good whack that made me see little whirling things around my eyes. My first reaction after recovering from whirling stars was rage. I made a flying leap at him, somewhat aided by having one foot against the back wall of the horse shed. He had just turned to run when I hit him with a flying tackle at about shoulder height. We both went sprawling headlong about six feet into a bed of cinders just outside the horse shed. Since his face was in front of mine, he hit the cinders first with devastating results. His immediate squalling told me he had been hurt more than from the tackle, so I got up quickly and saw blood running from his face where it had been ripped by the cinders.

Of course, we had to report his condition to the teacher to get the bleeding stopped, and I expected to be expelled from school or severely disciplined, but every one of the boys in the horse shed, including the injured one, insisted he had tripped and fallen on the cinders all by himself. I did not thereafter have any more problems with that boy. As a matter of fact, a few days later he and his brother brought some real cigarettes from their father's supply and taught me how to smoke. It definitely was an act of currying favor with me, but whether they were really doing me a favor was beside the point at that time.

On a few rare occasions at the beginning of the winter season, we older boys were allowed to go rabbit hunting during the noon hour. The area around our schoolyard was somewhat brushy, and a few ditches nearby were overgrown with weeds and buckbrush. There were always rabbits to be found within minutes of the schoolyard. This was not to say that we very often caught one, although I'm sure the poor rabbits must have been scared half to death by a whole pack of yelling kids running after them and throwing clubs at them. One would think the rabbits would be scared all the way into the next county, but they always seemed to be back the next day.

One winter we had a teacher who even let us bring our dogs to school to help us with our rabbit hunts. Only one boy could bring his dog in any one day and tie him out in the horse shed until the noon hour. Most of the dogs would take off for home as soon as they were unleashed, but some would stay with us and help chase the rabbits. When it came my turn, I brought our old Airedale who was not a very good rabbit dog but was at least an avid hunter. When it came to the noon hour, I unleashed Old Dale, and he immediately raced down to the nearest ditch and started looking for rabbits. When our gang caught up with Old Dale, we saw him excitedly standing behind a clump of dead grass wiggling his short tail vigorously. Suddenly he pounced on the clump of grass and grabbed in his mouth a very scared rabbit. We immediately took the rabbit away from Old Dale but heaped great praise on him for his achievement. He was the only dog brought to school that succeeded in catching a rabbit. I can't recall him ever catching a rabbit anytime afterward.

My brother Del, being older than I and more interested in reading books, seldom played the same games in school as we younger fry. But there were a few occasions when he did participate in school activities. Two occasions stand out in my mind.

One bright sunshiny day when we were all out on the playground doing our thing, the older boys were off to themselves trying to figure out something interesting to do, while we younger kids were playing stick horse or hopscotch or some such trivial game. I wasn't paying any attention to what the older boys were doing so was somewhat surprised when one of them called out to me to come see what they were doing. They had Del by the arms holding him, and in the middle of the playground lying on the ground was Del's cap. The older boy said, "Hey, Don, you wanna go kick Del's cap around while we hold him?" I was a bit suspicious about this and was afraid they would turn him loose, but they assured me they would hold him until I got away. Del was straining at his captors and defying me to go near his cap. I was still suspicious, but the thought of getting even with Del for some of the mean tricks he had pulled on me was too strong. I raced out into the middle of the playground and gave the cap a big kick. The cap rolled off to one side, exposing a big heavy rock which was beneath the cap. Needless to say, I was in agony for the next several minutes while the older boys, including Del, clapped and

shouted in glee. As I said before, I was sort of a slow learner, but once I learned a lesson, it stayed with me a long time.

In a way this next tale may have been poetic justice, because Del was the butt of this prank. He had been writing a theme for one of his classes and was supposed to have it ready by a certain day. It was the night before the day it was due, and Del was working furiously to get the paper completed. Alas, he discovered some of the material he needed to finish had been left at the schoolhouse. The only way he could get the material was to call up the teacher and ask her if he could come got the key so he could get into the schoolhouse for the material. She was agreeable and told him to come on before she went to bed.

Del had to go to the barn and saddle up Old Mac, a long-legged brown mare which older brother Harold used as a buggy horse. When he was ready to go, he came to the house and begged me to go with him to keep him company. He would never have admitted to being the slightest bit afraid to go out on the dark road alone at night, but this night he wanted someone to go with him, even a younger brother who was more afraid of the dark than he. I didn't want to go, but he kept begging me and promising me all sorts of favors in return, so I finally reluctantly agreed and climbed up on the mare behind him. It was about three-fourths of a mile to the teacher's house and almost the same to the schoolhouse, but Old Mac was a very fast horse and soon made the trip. It was so dark out on the roads that we had to depend on the mare to follow the road because all we could see was the brushy fence rows on either side. By the time we got to the schoolhouse we were pretty well spooked by imaginary wild animals we might have encountered, so much so that I refused to get down off the horse and said I'd wait until Del had gotten the papers from the schoolhouse.

When Del stuck the key in the door, there was a blood-curdling squall from within, and a metal wastepaper can was hurled down the aisles, striking the desks on either side as it bounced along. I can vividly remember the hair rising up on my head, and my instinct to flee was very strong. Old Mac was frightened also and immediately whirled about to leave the premises. Since I was already on Old Mac and holding the reins there was nothing to stop us from racing out of the schoolyard and down the road. When I finally caught my breath and looked back to see where Del was, there he was pounding down the road behind us and gaining. I managed to stop the mare and let him on, and we raced on down the road to the nearest house to report what had happened.

While we were excitedly recounting our experience, we noticed the family trying to stifle their smiles, and when the back door opened and two grown neighborhood boys sneaked in, we knew we had been had. They had heard Del on the party line when he had called the teacher for the key and had sneaked down to the schoolhouse before we got there and hid inside. Everyone except Del and I had a big laugh, and we rather shamefacedly went back to the school and finished our interrupted trip.

You will note I was not greatly enthusiastic about my studies in this chapter, principally because I had not yet found a subject that interested me. Our teaching in this little country grade school was strictly the three Rs (Reading, Riting and Rithmetic). I make no apologies for the system because it did turn out students with a good basic background for further study, and many of the students who attended this little backwoods school went on to compete successfully with students from city schools and even earn college degrees.

I have said nothing of my experiences in the local high school which I attended. I will relate some of those activities in a later chapter.

Chapter V

Horse Power

My EARLIEST RECOLLECTION of horsepower (I may have been three or four years old) was the day I was kicked by a horse. Perhaps the incident stood out in my mind because of the violent nature of the experience. After all, when a very small boy gets swatted head over heels by a 1500-pound draft animal, he is impressed.

The incident occurred when I was watching the work horses coming into the barn lot below the house for a drink of water at the watering tank. We had no large ponds out in the pastures at that time from which the animals could drink, and all our livestock had to be watered from this tank. The tank had to be filled daily by pumping by hand large quantities of water from a well situated there.

I probably had a special interest in that tank of water because one of my first work assignments was to help keep that tank full of water each day. A visit by a bevy of horses or herd of cattle could empty the tank in a few minutes which had taken me what seemed like hours to fill. It was for just such an occasion that our work horses had come in to drink what had been so laboriously pumped.

There was one big old white horse that was sort of a kingpin of the group on account of his size and ability to use his heels to the best advantage. He had planted himself in front of the tank and wouldn't allow any of the other horses an opportunity to drink. When another horse would approach, he would reach out with his long neck and bare his teeth and try to take a bite out of the offender. There was no good reason for him

doing this since he had already drunk his fill, but I felt he was being very unfair about the matter. After watching this demonstration of selfishness for several minutes, I became so incensed at such injustice that I raced out of the yard and down to the tank, picking up a big clod on the way, and ran up behind the big horse and heaved the clod, hitting him squarely on the rump. Whether in retaliation or reflex action, the horse lashed out with both hind feet, hitting me squarely in the face and tumbling me head over heels. That last part I wasn't aware of because the next thing I knew I was sitting on my mother's lap on the porch of the house with cold wet cloths being placed on my face, but most frightening of all, I was unable to see. My eyes were completely closed from the swelling, and I was unable to see for several days afterward. Fortunately there was no permanent damage to my eyes. Apparently the hooves of the horse had struck the bones of my face and forehead without striking the eyes which could have rendered me blind.

Needless to say, I learned a very important lesson from that incident — horses are bigger than people, and if one wants to administer punishment to them, keep out of reach of those long hind legs. I had many occasions to remember that lesson when I became a little older and was required to drive horses and mules to pull farm implements.

I can't correctly say I was born into the horse-and-buggy age because the automobile had been invented and Henry Ford had initiated his assembly line production of Model T Fords. My father was one of the first in our community to have one of those noisy vehicles, probably because of the persistent urging of two teenage daughters, but when I came along we still had the usual horse-drawn conveyances and were using them quite regularly. The principal reason for their use was the fact that there were no hard-surface roads within almost 10 miles from our home, and the frequent rains and snows made our old yellow clay hills practically impassable for a motorized vehicle.

For family travel we had a two-seated surrey (without the classical fringe). As many as six could ride, providing there was some lap-sitting by small fry. This vehicle was usually drawn by two old, tired work horses that were so stiff and sore from pulling a plow or cultivator all week, that we seldom got to go any faster than a slow walk, maybe about five miles per hour. Sometimes if the road was dry and we were descending a long steep hill, the tired old horses would break into a stodgy trot, kicking up clouds of dust which went directly into the surrey, covering all occupants with a thin layer of dust. This downhill jouncing usually caused the release of flatulence from one or both horses, which gave the dust a rather characteristic aroma. This mode of family travel was standard practice in our community, especially during muddy road conditions, which in my memory seemed to be most of the time.

Another horse-drawn vehicle which we had on our farm and used only on special occasions was a buggy. This was a single-seated, four-wheeled vehicle with a canvas top which could be folded back at a rakish angle. It was lightly built and designed to be pulled by a single horse. A special horse was usually kept for this purpose, one that could trot very fast or one that could keep up a good steady pace for long periods of time. Our mail carrier and our doctor used these vehicles for their daily travels.

My brother Harold had a very fast and spirited bay mare which pulled the buggy when he went courting. He had the reputation of having the fastest buggy in the county. It was my greatest ambition to accompany him on one of his dates and ride like the wind in his fast buggy. Since I was eight years younger than he, the idea of taking me along was not especially favored. However, after much nagging, he finally agreed to take me on one of his Saturday night trips. As soon as we got over the first hill, he pulled out a couple of big "White Owl" cigars from his inside pocket and advised me that part of the procedure was to smoke a big cigar when going out with the ladies. Now smoking cigars or anything else was taboo in our family, and I was a bit taken aback to learn that my big brother had become such a sinful person, but since I had asked to go along, I felt I had no recourse except to conform with the rules. We fired up our stogies, and I managed to suppress my urge for violent coughing. About a half-mile down the road and one-fourth less cigar, I began to, as the saying goes, "turn a little green around the gills," and wished I hadn't started that cigar. Another half-mile and well short of the girlfriend's house, I wanted to give up the whole adventure. So my big brother and supposedly "Good Buddy" obligingly turned around and took me back home, just as he had planned to do in the first place.

Yet another horse-drawn wheeled vehicle in which we frequently traveled to pick up heavier supplies, such as lumber or coal for our stoves, was a big high-wheeled wagon which we referred to as the "big wagon." It had a sturdy open box-like bed made of top-grade oak lumber and could be fitted with side boards which essentially doubled the capacity. The only provision in this vehicle for human comfort was a spring-fitted wooden seat hooked over the sides near the front from which the driver could handle the lines to the horses and manipulate the brakes. Oh yes, this big cumbersome vehicle needed brakes to help control a runaway team or prevent a heavy load from running up on the horses' heels on a steep hill.

Occasionally when there was deep snow or mud axle-deep, the big wagon might be brought into use for taking the family to church or to town for supplies. Otherwise it was used principally on the farm for gathering corn, hauling out manure and sometimes for breaking a young mule to work as a team with another horse or mule.

Driving a team of horses was one of my greatest ambitions when I was too small to capably do so, but as I grew older and stronger my father gradually turned the lines over to me. I soon found this was not nearly as much fun as I had anticipated. I soon found myself spending hours and hours walking behind a harrow while driving a team of horses or riding on a corn cultivator in the hot sun driving a team of horses. My father was only too happy to turn that kind of driving over to me.

Nearly all farm production in our community was done with true horse power. The soil was plowed, disked and harrowed with horses, the seed was planted with horse-drawn implements, and nearly all the harvesting was done by horse-powered equipment. Only the actual threshing of grain was done by steam-powered equipment. Because of this dependency upon and close association with horses, we became intimately acquainted with each animal's personality and idiosyncrasies. Each animal had its own name and recognized that name when spoken to. For example, there was Old Maude. For some strange reason all our horses' names were preceded by the term "old." Maybe it was because most of them were advanced in years, but even younger horses coming under our care were referred to as "old."

Old Maude was the malingerer. She would slowly inch back as she was pulling a load along with another horse until her singletree would rest against the doubletree, thereby lessening the amount of work she had to do and force her teammate to pull harder to make up for her deficiency. Such shirking of duty was very annoying to me and sometimes caused me to use some words not at all acceptable in our family. If I didn't watch her constantly and keep yelling her name and smacking her with the lines, she would repeat this stunt all day long.

One of our neighbors told us a story of his young son reporting a new naming of their horses. It seems the boy had been tagging along behind a hired hand as he worked a team of horses. The hired hand had not grown up in our Puritan-like community and sometimes used language not readily condoned by the elders. One day at noon when the family and the hired hand were all sitting at the table eating their dinner, the young son loudly announced the horses now had new names. Old George was "Old Son-of-a-Bitch," and Old Mollie was "Old Biscuit Ass." Needless to say, there was some embarrassment all around the table.

Old Nell was blind. Several years before I was old enough to know about such things, an epidemic of periodic ophthalmia (moon blindness) afflicted many horses in the community, and some were rendered completely blind. She was one of the unfortunate ones. Nevertheless she was a very willing worker and would keep up her end of the load all day long. I always felt very sorry for her and would give her an extra portion of grain in the evening after work. She had adapted very well to her blindness and could find her way around the barnyard and into her stall without running into anything. When the horses were turned out to pasture at night for grazing, she would follow one of the other horses to avoid falling into some of the ditches which, of course, she couldn't see.

Old Prince was aptly named. He was a prince of a fellow and my favorite horse. He had no bad habits and would uncomplainingly go about his daily work without shirking. He was always very considerate of other farm animals and the bare feet of small boys. Our old dog Dale, sensing this characteristic, would curl up in front of Old Prince in the stall within inches of those huge feet and spend the night there. They became very close friends, and many evenings in the summertime when the horses would be turned out to pasture for the night, I would see Old Dale trotting along beside Old Prince as they went out to explore the far reaches of the pasture.

Then there was Old Topsy. She came to us by way of a horse trader, and we didn't know much about her idiosyncrasies until we had worked her awhile. She had a brand of some kind on her left hip which led us to believe she had been used as a western cow pony. We wondered at the time why the cowpokes had sold her for common farm work, but we were to find out later there was a reason. Old Topsy was very unpredictable in the harness and would sort of pull in spurts. She would lunge forward to get the load started, then stop until her teammate caught up, then lunge ahead again. This would go on for some

60

time until she decided this trick would not get her out of the work at hand, and she would become a rather decent work horse.

My brother Del and I soon discovered another characteristic of Old Topsy. As a cow pony she had been taught to stand still out in the pasture so a person could walk up to her and catch her. After we had discovered this unique characteristic, we would take turns boosting each other up on her back and galloping around the pasture. We didn't have a bridle or reins. We just rode bareback and used a stick to guide her by tapping her face on one side or the other. After a short time we soon discovered another quirk in Old Topsy's nature. When she became tired of this galloping around, she would suddenly plant her feet and stop so quickly that whoever was riding would go flying off over her head. One such experience I had with this caper was for me to fall out in front of her, and her momentum was too great for her to stop so she leaped over the top of me, barely missing me with her hind feet as she came to the ground. That was enough for me and I was ready to quit. But Del said he wasn't afraid to ride her, so he climbed up on her and started racing her around the pasture. Old Topsy soon decided she's had enough and galloped straight toward a barbed wire fence. She stopped just before she hit the fence, and Del went flying over her head, just barely clearing the fence — all except for one big toe which caught on the barbed wire and ripped a big gash in it. We had to go to the house to get the toe wrapped up, and the whole story came out. Needless to say, we never got to ride Old Topsy "free will" in the pasture again. We finally figured out why those cowpokes out west had sold Old Topsy for a plow horse.

We had two other horses that were considered to belong to my older brother Harold. They were light-boned and very fleet of foot, suitable for driving to a buggy or riding to high school. The first one my father purchased for Harold was Old Mac. You have met Old Mac before in these pages, one night at the schoolhouse when Del and I went after some papers. Old Mac was a long, lean, brown mare, very fast but very difficult to ride in a trot. She took long, far-reaching strides which were fine as a buggy horse, but to an uninitiated rider it was almost traumatic. Her bounce could rattle your teeth and settle your spine if you didn't know how to pump in the saddle.

There was one episode when someone was allowed to ride Old Mac who didn't know how to pump or hardly how to ride. The results could have been tragic. It was in the summertime, and my nephew Gwendle was riding Old Mac to carry drinking water to the threshing crew that was at our place that day. He came back to the house for a fresh supply of water and a brief rest while he chatted with some of the neighborhood kids who had come with their parents to help with the threshing day activities. One of the neighborhood girls there that day

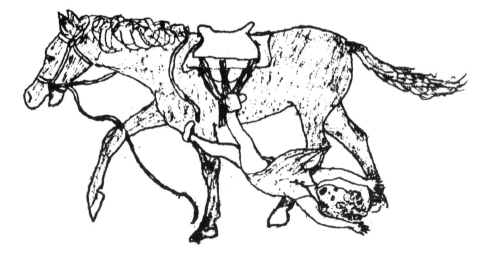

kept nagging Gwendle to let her ride Old Mac. Finally he agreed and went out and helped her get into the saddle. Things might have been different if this had been a regular saddle, but it was an English saddle without any horn or anything to hang onto in case one was about to fall off.

After the girl got into the saddle, she slapped Old Mac with the reins and went jolting off over the hill. Gwendle returned to the porch and sat down, waiting until the girl returned with Old Mac. Suddenly he heard her screaming, "Whoa, whoa, whoa," and looked out to see Old Mac come jolting down our hill toward the barn lot gate with the girl bouncing about six inches high after each contact with the saddle. She soon lost her balance and went tumbling over the side of the horse. Unfortunately her foot got caught in a stirrup, and she was being jerked along upside down along the roadway. When Gwendle saw what was happening, he raced across the yard and cleared the yard fence with a flying leap to come to the rescue. Unfortunately when he landed on the other side of the fence, his bare foot hit a stob (a stick or piece of wood sticking out of the ground). The rescue efforts ceased immediately while Gwendle howled and held his foot. Fortunately Old Mac had to stop at the barn lot gate because it was closed, and some of us were able to get the girl extricated from the stirrup. As I recall, she was mostly scared and a little bruised but not nearly as badly hurt as her rescuer.

The second horse my brother Harold had was Mickey. We didn't call her "Old" Mickey because she was a young, very spirited mare that just didn't qualify as being old. She was a beautiful, light tan mare that would proudly prance about and hold her head and tail very high when she was being ridden. She was far too fragile and spirited to ever attempt to use her as a plow horse, and as soon as Harold went off to college she was sold. Probably my father figured she was far too dangerous to let Del and me ride her.

Later on when Del started to high school, my father purchased a saddle pony from my sister Vera and husband John, which was to serve as transportation to high school, first for

Del and later for me when I was ready for high school. The pony was the offspring of an old saddle mare which Vera and John kept for their children to ride. The colt was named Charlie after an old Negro hired hand who worked on the same ranch as did John.

We purchased this pony as a four-year-old and had to break it to ride, which wasn't difficult because it had already been handled a lot as a colt. Charlie turned out to be a very talented, five-gaited saddle horse with which we were to have many happy and sometimes exciting experiences. More will be said about these experiences in a later chapter.

I would be remiss if I didn't relate something of the long, tedious days of working with our farm horses. Most of my recollections were those of the long, tedious days of preparing the soil for planting and cultivating the crop after it was up. My first job with a team of horses was to harrow the ground to break up the clods. Sometimes I could ride on a board laid across the two sections of the harrow, but most of the time I had to walk behind the harrow, with clouds of dust billowing up into my face. The reason I couldn't ride all of the time was because my weight on the harrow would cause the teeth to dig in too deeply and drag up large quantities of dirt and debris which had to be dug out from beneath the harrow.

After the ground was properly prepared, my father would use a horse-drawn planter to plant the corn or soybeans. I was never allowed to do the planting because all the rows had to be kept straight and evenly separated for later cultivation. But there were always other fields to be harrowed and disked while my father was doing the planting, thereby keeping me busy and allowing no time for fishing.

Later on when the crops came up, the riding cultivator came into use. This was a two-wheeled implement fitted with two sections of little plow shovels which could be manipulated to plow out the weeds between the rows of corn or beans without digging up the crop itself. The team of horses had to be well trained to walk exactly in between the rows so as not to step on the plants and to keep the cultivator from getting off course. A pair of lines had to be looped over the shoulders of the driver to make sure the horses did stay in proper alignment. After about two or three days of this, both driver and team became very tired of this operation and spent more and more time resting under any available shade tree bordering the field.

I felt very sorry for our poor old work horses during these days. The cultivating work came during some of the hottest days of the year, and the relentless sun would beat down on the backs of the horses, as well as the driver. A sort of lather would form wherever the harness came in contact with the animal's body. This was especially true under the horses' collars, and a maceration of the skin occur at the point of greatest pressure. This was called galding and resulted in big open sores on some of the horses' shoulders. I could hardly bring myself to put a heavy collar on top of one of those open sores, but the farming had to be done, and we didn't have enough horses to let the injured animals go free until they were healed.

To make matters worse for the poor horses, this was also the season when hordes of biting insects were being hatched out. The most troublesome ones were the ever-present stable flies. These blood-sucking insects would follow the horses to the field in the morning and stay with them all day long, swarming around their legs and under their belly. Periodically they would stick their needle-like bill into the skin of the horse, occasionally the driver, and get a small drop of blood. It wasn't so much the amount of blood they took, but it was that stinging bite that hurt. I know first-hand about that. We didn't have any modern insecticides at that time to control these pests, so the poor horses just had to give up and let them bite.

Another more vicious bloodsucker was the horse fly. There were two or three different species of these, the largest one being fully an inch long. They seemed to appear out of nowhere and land on the horse's back or along the neck where the horse couldn't reach them with his teeth. These giant insects would quickly sink their knife-like bill deeply into the horse's skin and start drawing out relatively large quantities of blood. The horses would twist and squirm and try to bite at the offenders, but the evasive critters would eventually get a bellyful. When more than two or three of these insects were attacking my team, I would stop the horses and sneak around very quietly and slap the offender hard enough to squash him and get a hand all covered with blood. If I could get in a good position to swing my good right fly-catching hand, I might be able to capture the culprit without squashing it. If I were successful, I would gleefully make an example of it by sticking a rather long wheat straw or thin dried weed through the insect's tail end and turn him loose. If my wheat straw wasn't too heavy, I would have the pleasure of seeing the rascal take off very slowly, barely gaining altitude, as it disappeared over the next hill. I never knew if it gave warning to its brothers and sisters and others of its kind whenever it went back to wherever it came from, but it seemed to me we never did have as many horseflies afterward.

A discussion of horsepower on the average Midwestern farm would not be complete without giving credit to another species of four-legged energy. This was the Missouri mule. The state became noted for its production of mules and outstripped all other states in production of the critters.

It is not exactly correct to say a mule is a different species than the horse. Actually a mule is part horse, being the off-spring of a mare and a jack. I once heard a geneticist describe a mule as being an "illegitimate son of a jackass, without hope of posterity." This is essentially true. It is a rare occasion in nature when two separate species can crossbreed and produce a true hybrid. But nature didn't bend far enough to allow the hybrid mule to reproduce itself, therefore no hope of posterity.

Mules are very strong and tough, and it has been said they were instrumental in the Allied Nations' winning World War I. Mules were used in large numbers to pull artillery through the mud of France, thereby placing the Allies in key positions. After the war was over, it was believed the mule would revolutionize farming and replace the horse as a draft animal. They did to a certain extent, but along came the gasoline-powered tractor and replaced them both.

Shortly after World War I, my father decided he wanted to raise mules, not only for his own use but to sell to others to bring in a little extra income. He started with the old mares we had on hand for producing the mule colts and proceeded to grow them up to young adults and break them to harness for use as draft animals. This all sounds very simple and logical, but I can assure anyone that such was not the case. A mule can, all at the same time, be stubborn, mean and crafty. There is just no comparison between the intelligence of a horse and a mule. The mule would win hands down every time. I might even go so far as to say a mule might even rate higher than some people I have known. I have known some mules to so completely dominate their owners that they had to be sold because the owner couldn't control them. Not so with my father. He must have read or learned somewhere that mules had to be handled with a firm hand, because among the several mules he raised and broke to harness, he did not fail to be the complete master. Even a very young mule still suckling its mother would show its independence by refusing to go into its "keep" stall while its mother was being taken outside for farm work. My father soon remedied that problem by giving the youngster a resounding swat across the rear with a big paddle he kept handy for such purposes. This would send the young dissident flying into the stall twisting his tail in pain, and that would be the last time such treatment had to be administered for that purpose.

The paddle was kept on hand constantly because, as the mule grew older, he would get new ideas of resistance and have to be immediately shown he could not get by with it. I have seen my father step in behind a big 1500-pound mule that kept insisting on running out of a stall and whack him over the rump with that big paddle when the mule could have plastered my father against the opposite wall with one swift blow of his heels. Instead, the mule would cower in his stall until my father could put a halter on the mule's head and tie him in place.

To complete the job of preparing a mule for farm work, there had to be a breaking to the harness exercise. This was no small task and quite often was attended with much excitement and possible danger. As I said earlier, a mule can be stubborn, mean and crafty, either singly or all at the same time, and I have seen them exhibit all three in every phase of the breaking process.

The first phase is to get the harness on the mule. They are instantly suspicious of anything that touches them, especially their long, sensitive ears. In order to put on a bridle without taking it completely apart, it must be pulled over those long ears. Mere man is at considerable disadvantage because the mule can hold his head higher than one can reach. The only way is to grasp one of those long ears and pull it down far enough to get the bridle on halfway. Then when you let loose of the first ear to grasp the other, the mule casually flips his head and flings the bridle all the way into the next stall. In the meantime, he has managed to crowd you over against the side of the stall and step on your toes. Oh yes, he does it on purpose, too. After several tries one may succeed in getting the bridle on, but then comes the exciting part — trying to throw all that heavy harness and rattling chains up on his back. Add terror to all his other characteristics, and you have a "whirling dervish" on your hands. The only hope is to hold some of the harness up there until the mule decides it isn't going to hurt him and will settle down enough for the full set to be put in place. This isn't all there is to it. There is a cinch strap or belly band hanging down on the other side that has to be pulled over and fastened, and just the act of stooping over and reaching under his belly for the strap may get your head kicked off. It is best to have a stiff wire with a hook on the end to slip under there and slowly pull the strap toward you. Then comes the crupper. To you city folks, the crupper is an important adjunct to any good set of harness. It is a rolled leather strap that has to be placed under the tail of the animal being harnessed so as to keep the harness in place. Now to a mule, the tail is also a very sensitive appendage, and just to take hold of his tail is an exciting adventure in itself, but putting something under that tail is something else. Could be that such is the reason for our having a couple of sets of harness without cruppers.

After spending all this time getting the mule harnessed, we knew the real fun was yet to come — getting him out of the barn and hitching him alongside another animal, preferably a very calm and wise old horse with lots of experience in breaking mules. Such a horse was Old Prince. You have met him earlier in these pages. He never seemed to get alarmed or excited. We could tie a stout rope to the hame on Old Prince's harness and then to the halter of the mule, and Old Prince would practically drag that mule out to the big wagon to be hitched as a team for the training session.

After all the snaps and tugs were properly fastened, we would climb into the wagon and say, "Git up," and Old Prince would obediently start forward. The mule, of course, had a different idea. He would go into a frenzy of twisting and turning and do his best to divest himself of the wagon and Old Prince.

We had one mule that actually got down on the ground and rolled under the wagon tongue and came up on the same side as Old Prince. We had to unhitch from the wagon and get everything straightened out before we could get back to the training session.

Throughout all these early antics, Old Prince would remain unperturbed and keep going forward and half dragging the mule until we got out into a plowed field or muddy road. After a half-hour or so of making the mule pull his share of that heavy wagon, we would return to the barn with a very tired and passive mule.

They don't all work out that easily. I remember one instance when we were taking a big black mule out for a training session, and we were going along a back road that was very deep with mud. The wagon was very difficult to pull with mud rolling up on the wheels, and the mule was getting a good workout. We figured we could soon go back home with the job all finished. About that time we came to a place along the road where the ditch on Old Prince's side of the road had been washed out very deeply, even encroaching upon the road. There are those who would say that what happened next was just a happen-so, but I saw the whole thing and believed it to be more than accident.

There was nothing on the mule's side of the road for him to become alarmed at, but just as we came alongside the deep ditch on Old Prince's side, the mule suddenly began crowding Old Prince toward that ditch. Poor Old Prince could see it coming, and he was doing some pretty fast back-pedaling to stay out of that ditch. For once I think Old Prince was becoming alarmed. The mule had the advantage. The mud was very slick, and the road sloped toward the ditch, and Old Prince was losing ground. Suddenly just before the inevitable happened, Old Prince reached over with his head and bit the mule right between the ears. The effect was instant and in time. The mule immediately ceased his shoving and got back on his side of the road and didn't try that stunt again. Thereafter I never doubted that some animals could reason when the occasion required.

I mentioned that one of the characteristics of a mule was his stubbornness. That trait was vividly demonstrated by one of our young mules in the final stages of being broken to the harness. My father had taken a team of horses and this young mule to the far pasture to do some plowing. The young mule was hitched between the two older horses in a three-abreast hitch so each animal was required to pull at least one-third of the plowing operation. The horses were old hands at this, having been conditioned to such heavy labor by weeks and months of strenuous work, whereas the young mule was not conditioned to such drudgery and greatly resented having to keep up with the older animals. For the first few hours he did a lot of prancing and twisting in the harness to show his displeasure.

It was about the middle of the afternoon when I saw my father coming over the hill toward the house leading the two horses, but the mule was nowhere in sight. When I asked where the mule was, he said in rather strong language for him that the mule had deliberately lain down in the harness and refused to get up. No amount of yelling or smacking with the lines could make the mule move. He had been forced to unhitch the horses and come in, leaving the mule there on the ground.

I had recently heard of a sure-fire method of making a balky mule move and was anxious to try it. I told my father I would get that mule up and proceeded over the hill to look for him. There he lay with every indication he intended to spend the night there. I yelled and kicked him in some of his most tender spots, but he just grunted and lay there. Now for my secret method: I went around and gathered up a lot of dead grass and dried weeds and carefully stacked it under his belly, reached into my pocket, pulled out a match and set fire to the dried grass. Immediately the fire flared up and started singeing a few hairs on the mule's belly. The mule pulled up his legs under him as though he were going to jump up, but instead he merely pushed himself away about two feet from the fire and continued to lie there. After two or three times of my moving

the fire to the mule's belly and his moving away from it, I became very frustrated, and finally in disgust and frustration grabbed the mule by the ear, put my mouth into the funnel-like opening and yelled as loud as I could. Talk about galvanized action — the mule nearly knocked me over jumping to his feet and racing off to the barn at a full gallop. That last stunt of mine apparently was the key to breaking his determination to outlast his human tormentors and probably prevented him from pulling the same stunt the next time he was made to do heavy work.

I once heard a story about the stubbornness of a mule that closely paralleled my experience, and I can't resist telling it at this point.

There was a farmer who raised mules, and he had sold one to a neighbor over in the next county and had guaranteed the mule to be a good worker. The next morning the neighbor hitched up the mule to a wagon and climbed into the wagon and said, "Giddy-up," and the mule just stood there. No amount of urging or switching would make the mule move. The neighbor was so disgusted he climbed down out of the wagon, went to the house, telephoned the previous owner of the mule and told him what he thought of him and the mule, and he wanted his money back. The first owner told him he just didn't know how to handle that mule and he'd come over and show him how.

Shortly thereafter, the first owner arrived, walked into the lot where the mule was still hitched to the wagon, picked up an old piece of 2x4 and hit the mule up beside the head with a solid whack, almost flooring the mule. He then climbed into the wagon and said, "Giddy-up," and the old mule walked right on out to the road with the wagon. The buyer of the mule was aghast and said, "Why did you have to do that?" The previous owner said, "Well, first you have to get his attention." End of story.

Missouri mules did have a place in history, and I was glad of the opportunity to experience a part of that. But, as the old saying goes, "I wouldn't have missed it for the world but wouldn't give a dime for the same thing again."

Chapter VI

Harvesting

ONE OF THE MOST IMPORTANT PHASES of any farming operation is the harvesting of crops. With modern equipment there isn't much to tell; the farmer climbs up into the air-conditioned cab of his monstrous combine which gobbles up the ripened crop, separates the straw or stalk from the grain and deposits the finished product into a truck ready to be hauled directly to market. All this is being done in one operation while the operator sits in his comfortable, air-conditioned cab and listens to his favorite ball game.

"Now when I was a kid," these operations were each done separately with much back-breaking labor involving the greater part of the summer and fall, sometimes even into the winter with corn gathering. I suppose if we had known about combines in those days we would have complained bitterly about all the hard work involved in our harvest, but we didn't and accepted the labor as part of our existence and even enjoyed the challenge.

The first field crop to be harvested was oats. We always grew a small crop of this grain to be fed to the horses during the winter months and to be ground into meal to mix with other ground grain to feed to our dairy cows. I called this a small crop; actually it was grown on eight to ten acres, and by the time the entire crop was manually handled two or three times, there was nothing very small about it. Oats is a quick-growing crop usually planted very early in the spring, sometimes before the frost is entirely out of the ground. Many farmers sowed their oats by hand, carefully walking over every area of the

field in a measured pattern so that seed would be distributed to every foot of ground. To do this they had to carry a supply of seed in a bag suspended over one shoulder by a strap or twine. The planting would start at one side of the field and continue in a straight line across the field, with the sower reaching into the bag every fourth step, getting a handful of seed and making a wide, sweeping arc with his arm, releasing even amounts of seed through his fingers.

I never did get proficient at this, principally because my father wouldn't let me do it. He was a master of seeding. He had a rhythmic step and expert manipulation of the seed that resulted in grain being distributed evenly to almost every inch of ground. He could carefully calculate every trip across the field so there were no missed spots or overlapping of seeded areas. The proof of his talent came several days later when the seed came up and the plants could be seen very clearly over the entire field.

Later on during my youth, my father purchased a new-fangled device for planting oats known as an endgate seeder. It was a mechanically operated machine which was attached to the rear end of the big wagon. There was a hopper into which the seed was poured, and when the wagon was pulled two little fan-like devices would fling the seed evenly behind the wagon. The mechanism was powered by a chain drive being driven by a sprocket attached to one of the rear wheels of the wagon. At the time, it was considered the ultimate in labor-saving devices, and many of the neighbors prevailed on my father to help them sow their oats with this new gadget.

After the seed oats were planted, they grew very rapidly to about two feet in height and developed seed heads that were ready for harvest sometime in late June. This did not mean they were ready to be threshed out for feed or seed. The plants were still somewhat green, and the grain needed further curing. The next stage was to cut the grain with a horse-drawn machine known as a binder. It got this name by reason of being able to gather a measured quantity of oat stems into a bundle and bind it with twine (naturally called binder twine). It was an ingenious implement for those times because it was capable of tying a knot around the bundle, cutting the twine and kicking the finished product out of the side of the machine. These were expensive machines, and most farmers could not afford to own one by himself unless he had a lot of farm land and considerable income from grain harvest. My father was able to have the use of this machine by making a joint purchase with a neighbor who had about the same acreage and then taking turns using it.

Cutting and binding the grain with one of these machines didn't mean that the job was done. Someone had to follow the machine on foot, pick up each bundle, carry to a centrally located spot and set them up in shocks of 10 to 14 bundles each. When my father was cutting his grain, the neighbor with half-interest in the machine would come help with the shocking, and when he was cutting his grain my father would help him with the shocking. Since my father had boys of varying ages who could run after the binder, we were sent to the neighbor's farm to substitute for our father.

The neighbor was a grouchy sort of fellow who was a meticulous worker and took pride in showing us boys how fast he

could work. When he was at our farm, he would challenge us to keep up with him and do just as he did. He would take off after the binder at a very fast walk, grabbing up bundles as he went and yelling at us boys to hurry up and get some bundles. We would have to run ahead of him to get our share of bundles. Then when we would get enough bundles to make a shock, we had to set them in exact position with the proper slope to shed rain. After the shock was made, we had to especially prepare two bundles to make a cap. This was done by hoisting up a bundle in front of the body, setting the heel in the groin and breaking down the heads of the bundle in such a way as to resemble a fan-like shape. A second cap had to be placed in the opposite direction to provide good coverage.

In the meantime, the binder being pulled by three big horses hitched abreast was moving on around the field at a fast clip, kicking out bundles by the dozens. The neighbor was a short, stocky man and could keep up a continuous fast pace. He enjoyed being able to outdo us and kept up a constant banter about my being so slow. One of my greatest secret ambitions was to be able to outpace that man and make him eat his words. It wasn't until I was a senior in high school before I could pull out ahead of him and watch him sweat and pant along behind without saying a word.

After the oats were all shocked and left to cure and mature in the field, we had to turn our attention to wheat. This crop was usually ready for cutting and shocking around the 4th of July, which often was the hottest time of the year. The bundles of wheat were much larger and heavier than oats, but by this time our muscles were hardened and accustomed to keeping up a good steady pace all day long. The neighbor, being on the heavy side, had to slow down in all the heat, and there was very little talk of how slow we boys were.

Very soon after the wheat was in the shock, the farmers in the community began talking about the final step which was threshing the grain. This was one of the big events of the year, both in financial return and social contacts. Most of the farmers in the community had banded together to purchase a threshing rig, which consisted of a huge black steam engine and a large, long metal monster of gears and flails called a separator. It was designed to gobble up the bundles of wheat or oats, shake them, beat them and sift them until the grain was removed from the stems, then blow all the chaff and straw out of a big long pipe called the blower. The power for all these whirling gears, beating flails and blowers was, of course, the huge black steam engine which was set facing the separator and connected by a big long belt. For some reason this belt had to be crossed in the middle. I never did know why except someone said if it weren't, the separator would run backwards and get everything all gummed up. This to me sounded something like the old gag of a left-handed monkey wrench.

The shareholders in this equipment had decided among themselves which ones were to be the engineers of this equipment. They had to be persons who had considerable knowledge of the machinery and its maintenance. Our nearest neighbor was selected to run the engine, and the grouchy fellow who worked with my father in cutting and shocking our grain was chosen to manage the separator. It was a good thing he was a grouchy person, because in this job strict compliance with the rules of feeding bundles into the separator was required. If some of the young bucks in the community started showing off by throwing in too many bundles at one time, the separator would become clogged and have to be cleaned out by hand. A good hard scolding by the separator man (straw boss) was usually sufficient, but sooner or later one of the boys would catch the straw boss looking the other way and clog the machine.

The threshing rig was moved from one farm to another,

and each member of the organization would take a team and wagon to haul in the bundles or send a stout young son to do the pitching of the bundles in the field. There was a great amount of competition among the young and old to see who could stack the most bundles on his wagon or pitch the fastest from the ground. Of course, if the young pitcher got too fast, the loader could always throw a few bundles off on the other side and tell the pitcher he missed some on the other side, thereby slowing him down when he had to go around on the other side to get them. If the bundle wagon loader got too ambitious and stacked his wagon too high, he might have an accident on the way to the machine by reason of losing about half of his load when crossing a gully in the field. In this case he came in for a lot of good-natured ribbing from everyone in sight. So there were some built-in controls on the over-enthusiasm of young crew members.

There was always a lot of kidding and prank-playing going on among the crew. Even the engineer, who was a pretty good prankster in his own right, would seize upon every opportunity to get off a good joke at someone's expense. He took

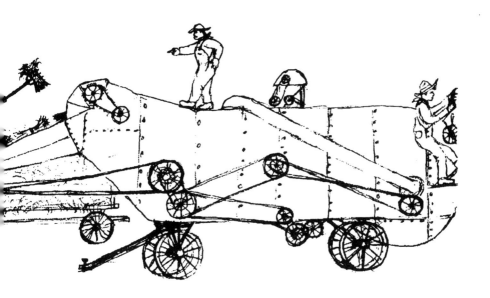

great pleasure in giving the big steam whistle a quick toot whenever someone with a skittish young mule pulled his loaded bundle wagon alongside the separator, resulting in a sudden departure of the mule, wagon and driver from the scene. His most favored stunt was to give a wet seat to an unsuspecting visitor. There were two big water reservoirs on the rear of the engine for purpose of providing water for steam production, and one could be filled from the other by opening a valve. Sitting on these reservoirs was a favorite spot for the old men of the community, and occasionally a political candidate from the county seat. The engineer usually kept a clean gunny sack on one of the reservoirs for that purpose.

When the unsuspecting visitor was peacefully settled in place and enjoying being a part of this entrancing operation, the engineer would surreptitiously start filling the reservoir being sat upon until the water began to overflow onto the surface. The water was usually lukewarm, and the victim was unaware that anything was wrong until he noticed a big dark spot creeping up on his pants at the crotch. Of course, the engineer would express great surprise that this happened and would start pulling levers and twisting valves in a great show of concern. In a couple of instances we had politicians to leave in a huff and never come back to our community again.

Most everyone following the threshing operation sooner or later found his niche in the day-to-day activities. Some preferred pitching bundles, others took great pride in operating a bundle wagon and stacking the bundles in just the right position to keep them from jostling off on the way to the separator. My father accepted the job of running the water wagon and helping both the engineer and the separator man when they needed an extra hand. Operating the water wagon was not a very difficult job ordinarily, but one in which punctuality was a must. If a steam engine with a hot fire going should run out of water, there could be irreparable damage. Sometimes my father had to go quite some distance to get clean water, and it required rather large quantities which had to be pumped by hand. There were a few times when he had to quit pumping before he had a full tank because he had heard the long-short blast of the engineer's whistle calling for water.

My father also had to be on hand to help every time the threshing rig was moved from one farm to another. As the unofficial assistant to the engineer and separator man, he had to help set the machine in exactly a level position and line up the big belt between the engine and the separator so it would stay on the pulleys.

My earliest job with the threshing operation was to carry drinking water to the workers in the field and around the threshing machine. A gentle old mare was saddled up for the occasion, and a big brown jug filled with cold water from the deep well in our front yard was hooked to the saddle with a leather strap. Our drinking water was very hard, meaning that it contained a high level of mineral elements. The water itself appeared crystal clear, but the workers went to great length complaining about the rocks I had in that jug and how the water rattled all the way down into their stomachs. They even complained that it rattled when they emptied their bladders. All this, of course, was just part of the bantering that went on among the workers, and it was all accepted as part of the fun of the threshing job. However, my water-carrying job was rather short-lived. I soon developed my own specialty with the threshing operation, and my nephew Gwendle took my place with the water jug.

My specialty started when the threshers were at our farm for their annual visit. My father wanted to build a straw stack over a framework of poles so that during the winter the livestock could get back under the straw stack for protection against the bitter winds and blowing snow. He wanted me to climb up on the rear end of the separator and manipulate the controls of the blower so the straw would be evenly distributed over the entire area of the stack and not be permitted to just pile up unevenly, which would allow rain water to penetrate the stack and cause rotting of the straw over the shelter.

The blower had hand-operated gears which one could manipulate and cause the blower to rotate back and forth across the stack and even gears to shorten or lengthen the big tube so as to distribute straw to the far side or to the near side. In order to take advantage of this maneuverability, someone had to stand up there on the end of the machine continuously and work the gears. There wasn't even a platform to stand on, just a narrow ledge created by a big angle iron brace holding the separator together. There was room only for one foot at a time on this brace; the other foot had to be cocked up on another protruding piece of framework.

I worked very diligently at this job because I thought it was quite an honor to be allowed to operate a part of this gigantic machine, even though it was just the tail end of the monster. It was a hot and dusty job that older members of the crew didn't want to do. The constant roar of the separator, the swirling chaff and dust from every crevice of the giant machine, the heat of the sun glaring down from overhead and reflecting back up from the galvanized surfaces and the awkward standing position made this job very uncomfortable.

When the threshing job was over and I crawled down off

my perch, I could hardly stand or walk because of the nerve-deadening effect of the constant vibration of the machine. My face and arms were covered with a thick layer of dust and chaff, with dark streaks around my eyes and down my face where the watering of my eyes and sweat from my forehead had soaked into the dust. I wasn't so sure I liked that job so well after all, but I was quick to recover when one of the older members of the crew came around and congratulated me on the good job I had done and offered to pay me two dollars to run the blower at his farm.

This was the beginning of my career with the community threshing crew. I was asked to run the blower at most of the farms in the community. There were times when I felt I was missing some of the better aspects of threshing by accepting this rather dirty, demeaning job when I could have been out with the big boys pitching bundles or even running a bundle wagon. But my position was a needed one and even commanded a little respect for my dogged determination to do the job well.

Not only were the men required for the threshing event, but the womenfolk would band together to help prepare dinner for everyone involved in the threshing operation. Such dinners were so lavishly prepared that they became somewhat of a legend in the folklore of the period. Each housewife had her specialty in which she took great pride and would insist she be permitted to prepare this particular item for the threshing table. Even a big bowl of mashed potatoes could be whipped to a peak of perfection, the melt-in-your-mouth kind, that other cooks could not attain. Other ladies were specialists in fried chicken, roast beef, corn on the cob, deviled eggs, dressing and gravy, pumpkin pie, chocolate cake — yes, I have seen all of these things on one table at the same time.

Each housewife serving as hostess to the threshers would try her very best to have a little more on the table than the other ladies. One lady whose home was one of the last to be visited by the threshers became so agitated by not being able to think up anything special for her dinner that hadn't already been done by the other ladies of the community, that she did the unthinkable — placed her best white linen tablecloth on the threshers' table that was to be sat around by sweaty men in dusty, grimy and oil-soaked work clothes. This was the coup d'etat that had all the other ladies gasping in disbelief. But just before the men came in to eat, the resourceful lady jerked up all the dinner plates and spread newspapers over the linen tablecloth all the way around the table, then reset the plates on the newspapers. The hungry threshers didn't notice a thing, but the ladies of the community talked behind their hand to each other for years to come about this breach of harvest table etiquette.

Later on in the year there were other harvesting tasks that were not as exciting as threshing, but necessary for the maintenance of the livestock during the winter months. Such a job was "putting up hay." This encompassed the cutting of green forage such as timothy, clover, lespedezia, alfalfa and various pasture grasses, raking and curing it in the field and finally hauling it to the barn to be hoisted up into the hayloft for the winter.

The hay had to be cut at just the right stage of maturity so as to have the maximum nutritional value and keeping properties. The cutting was done with a McCormick sickle bar mower pulled by a team of horses or mules. There was not usually much excitement about mowing a patch of forage for hay except an occasional encounter with a swarm of angry bumble bees when the horses and mower ran over their nest in the ground. The wise policy was to quickly throw the mower out of gear and yell "git" at the team. No further urging was needed, because by now the bumble bees were boiling around man and beast getting a sting in here and there. I have seen my father come in from mowing a clover field with his face all swollen from bee stings.

Once the nest has been discovered, the operator of the mowing machine will usually give the bees a wide berth the next time around, thereby leaving a patch of uncut hay to mark the spot where the bees' nest may be found. The very next Sunday afternoon these little patches of uncut hay became exciting entertainment for neighborhood boys.

There are several methods by which a nest of bumble bees can be eliminated, any one of which is fraught with excitement and even a little danger. One of the quickest methods is to burn them out. This is simply a matter of getting a pitchfork full of dry straw, setting it on fire, dumping the burning straw over the bumble bees' nest and running as fast as you can. The principle of this method is that the bees will swarm out of their nest into the fire and singe their wings so they can't fly. Unfortunately there are a few who are slow getting out of the nest and the fire has burned out, leaving these latecomers looking for someone or something to attack.

A second method is jugging. This is a very scientific method wherein a brown earthen jug is filled halfway up with water and stealthily set beside the opening of the bumble bees' nest. Then with a board or stick the ground is pounded very hurriedly around the nest, to be followed by a rapid exit to a safe distance. The principle here is that the bees will all come boiling out of the nest to look for enemies, and when they see none they will look for the opening to return to their nest. Being either nearsighted or stupid, they will see the dark hole of the jug and dive in to a watery reception. Theoretically, after things have quieted down one can go get the jug with a whole nest of bumble bees swimming around. Unfortunately some bees are

smarter than others and have found their own hole and are lying in wait for someone to come get their unhappy friends.

There is yet another more direct approach. This is the "whip 'em out" approach and is strongly advocated by any red-blooded country boy. First one must go down along the fence row and cut several bushes of buckbrush (no other kind will work), strip off all the leaves, select several stripped plants in each hand, carefully get down on your knees as if to pray next to the bees' nest, summon up a dose of adrenaline in your blood and start beating on the opening with both handsful of stripped brush. It pays to have a good loyal buddy to ward off attacks of some bees that might be returning to the nest or some that were not fully incapacitated by the switches.

There's really not much of a prize even if one were successful in whipping out all of the bees. There is only a handful of little honey cells, and most of these contain bee larvae. If one squeezes the whole packet, he might get a few drops of honey just for a taste. The real benefit is an afternoon of exciting adventure and the satisfaction of having rid the hayfield of these pests.

Getting back to haymaking, the cut forage should be well dried by now and ready to be raked up into windrows. This is accomplished by use of a two-wheeled sulky rake which has curved tines designed to pick up the loose hay and dump it in long rows around the field.

There are several methods of handling the hay at this stage, but in the early days we have two alternatives. Either we could pull it all up to a central spot in the field with a bullrake (a wide fork-like implement pulled by a horse at each end) to make a haystack, or it could be pitched up on a hay wagon to be hauled to the barn for storage. The latter method was used by my father because we had a big hayloft that would hold enough hay to carry our animals through the winter.

Getting the hay to the barn was easy. One person on a hay wagon would drive the team of horses alongside the windrows, and one or two men or boys with pitchforks would gather the hay into little stacks and throw it up onto the wagon, where it would be tramped into place by the loader to keep it from falling off on the way to the barn. It was always a source of considerable embarrassment for the loader to have the top half of the hay slide off on the way to the barn.

Getting the hay into the loft was a bit more complicated but was done with less manual labor. The loaded wagon would be pulled alongside the barn directly beneath the big yawning door leading into the hayloft. There was a special rigging of ropes and pulleys at the very peak of the barn which would permit a special tonged steel fork to be pulled down to the load of hay. The tongs would be plunged deeply into the load of hay and a triggering device set so the hay would stay on the fork until it got into the loft at the proper location. Then the man on the wagon would pull a little trip rope that was attached to

the fork and allow the hay to fall from the fork.

Of course, there had to be a source of power to hoist that large forkful of hay up into the gable of the barn and pull it on back into the barn on a steel rail. That power was usually supplied by a gentle old mare hooked to a very long rope extending from the rear of the mare through a series of pulleys up to the rear gable of the barn and out the loft door to the heavy fork that pulled up the hay. At the word "all right," a small boy, usually me, would start leading the gentle old mare across the barn lot, causing the hay to start rising from the wagon. Usually five or six big forksful would clean off the wagon. Another member of the family, usually Del, had to be up in the loft watching to see where to drop the hay so as to have an even filling of the barn loft. At his signal of "dump," the man on the wagon would pull the trip rope, and down it would come but would have to be rolled into position and tramped by the loft man. The unfortunate person in this whole operation was the loft man with temperatures of 110 to 115 degrees under that tin roof. Of course, if he didn't do such a good job of placing the hay in the right spot, no one could see until it was too late to do anything about it.

Another harvesting job we had at our farm was filling the silo. Not many farmers in our community had silos because silage (ensilage) was fed principally to dairy cows, and dairying was not commonly established in our area. Since my father had several dairy cows, he would have the silo filled each year by a crew from another community. About the only part we played in this operation was "tromping" the silage in the silo.

The operation consisted of men with teams and wagons going into the cornfield about roasting ear stage, cutting the cornstalks about four to six inches from the ground, loading the stalks into the wagons and hauling them to the cutter to be chopped and blown into the silo. The cutter was a very powerful and noisy machine, being belt-driven by a big tractor or steam engine. It could chop up a whole bundle of corn stalks at one time and propel the cut corn up an eight-inch pipe to the very top of the silo. The silage came down into the silo by way of jointed pipes which could be disjointed one by one as the silo filled.

Since it was essential that the silage be evenly distributed and closely packed inside the silo, my brother Del and I were assigned to handle this end of the operation. We took turns moving the downspout around over the inside area of the silo, and the other would follow the movement of the spout and "tromp" the silage in place. As the silage piled higher, we would remove a section of the pipe and let it down the silo chute with a rope. It quite often required two days to fill the silo, and by that time Del and I were quite tired of our job and were given to quarreling. However, at the finish it was exhilarating to peer out of the very top of the silo and see the whole countryside as would an eagle on a high perch, but it was also a chilling experience for me to look down at the ground from such a height. I guess I hadn't or never will get over that frightening experience of climbing down off that second-story porch roof.

The ground-up green corn soon began to ferment and continued to do so until there was sufficient buildup of acetic acid in the silage to stop bacterial action. Otherwise the silage would rot and be unfit for feed. As I mentioned earlier, the cattle dearly loved this fermented forage, and it provided a form of highly nutritious forage during the winter when there was no other green stuff available.

I recall an amusing incident in our silo one Sunday afternoon. A neighboring boy was visiting our home and kept wanting to climb up in the silo. The farm where he lived didn't have a silo, and he had never been inside one. I didn't think this was a particularly interesting thing to do, but I did take him up the ladder chute. I even took a bit of pride in being able to quickly climb to the highest rung without a bit of hesitation, while my friend was scared spitless with each step toward the top. The silo had just recently been filled, but it had settled down several feet below the top door, making it necessary for us to drop down into the silo. When we did so, we frightened a mouse which had also gotten in through the door and couldn't get out. We, of course, attempted to catch the mouse alive and chased it around the silo several times. The mouse became so desperate to find a hiding place that suddenly it ran toward my friend and ran up his britches leg. The contortions, screeching and stomping that took place would rival some of the modern rock 'n' roll. I'm sure a similar incident must have been the inspiration for jitterbug dancing. The poor boy had his britches all the way down to his ankles before the mouse jumped out.

After I quit laughing, I managed to dispose of the mouse with the silage fork which was kept up there.

One of the last harvesting chores of the season was gathering corn. This was usually put off until after the fall plowing was over and the ears of corn were completely dried out. A good hard frost was considered essential to curing out the corn. Consequently our corn gathering was quite often done on cold frosty mornings before the ground thawed out.

There was no machine to gather the corn in those days. We had to harness a team of horses, hitch them to the big wagon and slowly work our way through the field, grabbing ears from two or three rows as we went. Handling those frosty ears of corn even with gloves was a painful experience. The gloves would soon become soaking wet from the melting frost, and the cold air would almost literally freeze the gloves to our hands. Since this was the time of year when Del and I were in school, we didn't have a lot of corn gathering to do except on Saturdays, but that was enough to convince us that farming was not all fun and games. Our father had to keep up this corn gathering day after day until it was all in the barn. I have seen his hands all cracked and bleeding from the wet, cold conditions he had to endure.

Chapter VII

The Great Depression

IN THE LATE 1920s AND EARLY '30s the country suffered a financial recession greater than any it had ever experienced in its history. It soon became known as the "Great Depression." Farmers lost their land, small town banks closed their doors, industry slowed to a snail's pace, millions of laborers were out of work, bread lines and soup kitchens were a fact of life, and eventually the entire economy began to crumble. Even the high-rolling Wall Street tycoons began jumping out of their penthouse windows. Some economists are still debating why it happened, but one needs only to go back to grass roots problems for an answer. I say "grass roots" advisedly because that was literally where the trouble began.

Farming in those days was, and still is, the largest industry of the nation. More people were living on farms in the early '20s than in all the cities of the nation combined. But things were not going good out there on the farm. Very soon after World War I there was an inflationary period when prices for everything were skyrocketing, including land prices. Farmers were getting good returns for their crops and livestock. Everyone was euphoric about the future. Many farmers, including my father, bought more land and equipment to expand their operations, mortgaging their home place at high interest rates to do so. Younger farmers went deeply into debt to buy their way into the business. Soon farm products were flooding the market and prices began to fall. In order to meet mortgage payments, farmers put out more crops and grew more livestock to make up the deficiency. Naturally prices fell even farther until there was literally no market over cost.

When farmers couldn't meet their obligations to small town bankers who had loaned them money, foreclosures on farms began. When small town banks began having cash flow problems, the larger banks and moneyed interests began looking at those worthless notes and began pulling their money from the small town banks. Thus began a series of small town bank closings that caused people to have serious doubts about all banks. The end result was a run on all banks across the nation, causing wholesale closures until finally President Franklin D. Roosevelt was forced to declare a "Bank Holiday" which meant closing all banks until provisions could be made for government backing.

Meanwhile, back out on the farm, my father and about 75% of all farmers in our community had lost their farms. They were the first domino to go down in this series of financial disasters across the land. Most of the farmers losing their farms took advantage of the Federal Bankruptcy Act which left them with a few livestock, some farm machinery and horses to start over again on a rented farm. Not so with my father. He being what he thought a true Christian should be refused to take advantage of the bankruptcy act. He felt it was immoral to try to get out of a debt he had incurred and had given his word to repay. He made a trip to see the officials of the land bank with whom he had the loan and advised them of his inability to meet his obligations and told them to go ahead and take everything he owned.

The bank officials were much surprised at this attitude and suggested they take a little more time to consider the matter. They already had thousands of redeemed acres on their hands and really didn't want more if there were any way to avoid it. Finally they asked my father if he wished to stay on the land and pay what he could toward the obligation. My father readily agreed to this rather loose arrangement to give him a chance to maintain his personal sense of integrity. Eventually he was able to settle the loan agreement with the lending agency by their depreciating the amount of the loan to the then current land prices and he giving over the farm.

In an effort to meet his obligations, my father decided to go into the dairy business and sell cream to a distant creamery. This was an entirely new mode of farming for my father, and there were no other farmers in the community doing this. However, he had read about the success of the dairy business in his farm magazines and had seen ads offering young dairy calves for sale at a much reduced price in the state of Wisconsin. He decided this was the most economical way to get into the dairy business.

The breed of dairy calves my father decided upon was the Guernsey breed. They were very beautiful animals with a soft coat of tan hair with large patches of white scattered irregularly over their body. They were reputed to be very heavy milk producers as compared to the Jersey breed, which everyone in our community thought of as the true dairy cow. The Holstein breed had not yet been established in this country and would not have been a satisfactory breed for my father's business anyway because they produce milk with very little butterfat, and that was the product we intended to sell.

When we received our shipment of little female calves from Wisconsin, we found them to be much younger than we had anticipated, and they were still being fed whole milk. Since we were not yet in the dairy business and had only enough milk for our table use, we had to start feeding these baby calves a diet of corn and oats. This was quite a radical change for these delicate little calves, and most of them developed a diarrhea which lasted for a considerable length of time. The result was a stunting of the calves' growth from which most of them never fully recovered. But eventually they did reach maturity and began to produce calves of their own.

Unfortunately our little dairy enterprise fell victim to another problem. There had been a disease of mature dairy cows in the state of Wisconsin known as contagious abortion or commonly known as Bang's disease. It was an infection that would establish in the uterus of a pregnant cow and frequently cause an abortion of the developing fetus. Such a calamity would not only cause the loss of the calf, but would so disrupt the natural preparation of the mother for renewed milk production that there would be a greatly reduced milk flow afterward. This, of course, was what we were depending upon for an income from the enterprise.

This disease proceeded to spread through our herd, affecting cow after cow until we practically went out of business because of the loss of calves and poor milk production. There was no known cure for the disease. As a matter of fact, it had never been heard of in our community. Apparently we had brought the disease to our farm with the calves we had purchased in Wisconsin. We continued to struggle along with the limited production from our cows for another year and until it was time for them to give birth to another calf.

Happily in this year's time the cows had developed an immunity to the disease which permitted them to carry their calves to full term and come into full production. The calves were healthy, and we had plenty of milk to feed them.

One of my jobs in this dairy enterprise was to teach the baby calves to drink from a bucket. This was necessary for two reasons: first, the cow gave far more milk than the calf could safely consume, and secondly, we wanted all that milk to separate the cream from it to sell. The calf could have all the skim milk he wanted. There was no sale for the skim milk in our community, so we fed it to calves, pigs and even the chickens.

A baby calf is very difficult to teach to drink from a bucket. The natural inclination to hold his muzzle up while nursing is

just the opposite of holding his head down to drink. We would entice the calf to start sucking our fingers by first dipping them in the bucket of milk, then holding them out for him to get a taste of milk. This would cause him to grab our fingers with his mouth and start sucking vigorously. We would then hold up the bucket with one hand and pull the calf's nose into the milk with the hand he was sucking. Pushing his head down would immediately throw his nursing reflex out of gear, and he would jerk his head out of the bucket. But after a few more tries and the calf got a big swig of the warm milk, one could remove the fingers from his mouth but would have to continue holding his head down into the bucket for a few feedings until the calf was trained. It was also a good idea to stand back away from the bucket as far as possible because young calves have an instinct to give their nose a big hunch forward when they are nursing or drinking from the bucket. In the case of bucket-fed calves, the uninitiated bucket holder could get a whole lapful of sloshed-out milk.

As I said previously in this chapter, hard times started much earlier on Midwest farms. As I recall, my entire childhood was a succession of deprivation, but since I had never experienced anything differently, I didn't realize any particular hardship until I became old enough to get out into the world and see how city folks lived. We always had plenty to eat since we grew our own vegetables, picked our own fruit, raised our own meat and always had plenty of milk and eggs. Some of the townspeople who came to our country church dinners often commented that we "lived like kings," but they could not see that my mother was wearing undergarments made of feed sacks and that we boys were sleeping on straw ticks. To you city-bred folks, straw ticks are big cloth bags filled with straw to serve as mattresses. Of course, the feminine members of the family got to sleep on feather beds, but again we had to raise our own feathers.

Toys were out of the question, even at Christmas time. When I came along, there was an old battered toy box of a few pieces of tinkertoys, a few well-worn blocks and an old spring-wind top that still worked, all from a more affluent past. Occasionally my father would buy some oranges to put in our Christmas stocking. I had never been taught there was such a thing as a Santa Claus. Our parents believed only in the birth of Christ and that we should go to church on Christmas Day and celebrate that event. But I had heard lots of stories from other kids about a mythical Santa Claus coming down one's chimney and leaving toys for all good little boys and girls.

Not to be left out on such a happy possibility, I dutifully hung up one of my longest stockings. Big brother Harold decided it was time to let me in on the facts of life regarding Santa Claus. So after I had gone to bed he slipped in and left me a present. The next morning, Christmas Day, I raced downstairs to see if there was anything in my stocking. Sure enough, there was something in there, but to my dismay it was a dirty old pig's tail he had picked up from the last butchering. That broke me of believing in Santa Claus but not my spirit. The very next Christmas I gave Harold a very lavishly wrapped box containing another pig's tail from the current year's butchering.

Since we didn't have money for toys, we sometimes made our own. I once made a Santa Claus jumping jack as my Christmas present. I copied on cardboard a big picture of Santa Claus from one of our magazines and colored it the traditional colors with my crayons. I drew the arms and legs separately from the body, and after cutting out my pictures fastened the arms and legs to the body with clips I had brought from school. I then fastened

Rear view

string to each appendage in such a way that when pulled the arms and legs would jump up and down. So successful was this

98

enterprise that I kept it year after year and would bring it out each Christmas for my nephews and nieces to play with.

I think my favorite homemade toy was a rubber-band-powered tractor. It didn't faintly resemble a tractor, but it had a pulling and climbing power that was amazing. My brother Del first made this toy from a drawing he had seen in a book or magazine. It was made with a wooden sewing spool, a kitchen match, two thin pieces of hand soap and a rubber band. The two thin pieces of soap were placed on each end of the spool. They had holes through them for the rubber band to be attached to a short match stick on one end and a full length match on the other. When the full length match was rotated several times around, the rubber band would twist on itself inside of the spool and provide the power to drive the spool forward. It was an ingenious device for demonstrating several principles of physics but, of course, our only interest was in seeing it work. The soap would slow down the unwinding of the rubber band, and since the match was braced against the floor, the spool would slowly propel itself forward. Notching of the outer edges of the spool would give the toy extra climbing power. We spent many hours playing with this mechanical wonder and, of course, replacing the broken or worn-out pieces of soap.

We always had lots of empty spools around our house since our mother did her own sewing with an old treadle sewing machine. As with the above make-believe tractor, anyone with a little imagination could envision many things that could be done with spools. They could be pulleys for a make-believe threshing machine, a spindle for a miniature windmill, wheels for a toy wagon or car, and with a little whittling and a stick, made into a very functional top for spinning with thumb and finger.

Perhaps the most often made toy by me from these spools was a little make-believe truck. Using just a simple flat piece

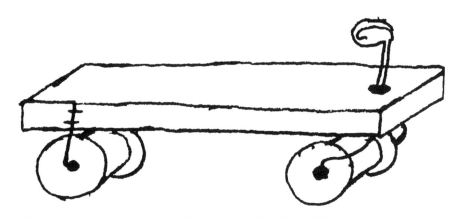

of board, some wire and two spools, I could concoct a reason-
able (at least to me) likeness of a truck. The rear wheels were
simply a wire put through the hole in the spool and bent to
come up the edges of the board and stapled in place. The front
wheels were more difficult. The wire had to be bent so as to
extend through a hole in the front end of the board and made
so the front wheels could be guided by the make-believe steering wheel. I had at least two or three of these so that when
neighbor kids or my nephew Gwendle came to visit, each of us
would have a truck to drive over our little dirt roads. We had a
play area under a big maple tree that had winding roads, hills
and even bridges for our trucks. We could spend many hours
at this kind of play.

Unfortunately there were some less happy times in the difficult years. Our mother had to do the work of two people to
keep us fed, washed and clothed. In order to keep up, she had
to have help quite often with some of her activities. These were
over and above the daily chores I wrote about earlier.

One hated job from my point of view was the weekly wash.
I have already mentioned the amber-colored water from the
kitchen pump which we could not use for washing our clothes,
and the water in the deep well in the yard was too hard for
homemade lye soap. So each wash day someone (guess who)
had to carry several buckets of water from the well down in
the barn lot. This well had water from the run-off of the barn
and was relatively soft water. The water was put in an old cop-
per wash boiler and heated on the stove. Extra water had to

be carried for the rinse water.

After the water was hot and the clothes all gathered together, the washing job began. Our washing machine was an archaic old hand-operated washer that required constant pushing and pulling of a handle to run the agitator. We had a gasoline-powered washer sitting in one corner of the wash house that had been used in years past, but the gasoline engine had quit, and we couldn't afford to have someone come fix it. I kept trying to get the old engine to run when I didn't have anything else to do but didn't know enough about engines to know why it wouldn't fire. I would have given my favorite pocket knife to have gotten that engine working and me away from that push-pull operation.

A companion job to that old washing machine was the butter churn. We didn't make butter every week, but it seemed to me the job came too often. It too was a hand-operated job. Our churn was designed to handle about two gallons of cream, and before we got our dairy herd it would require several days to save that much cream. In order to keep the cream from spoiling in hot weather it might have to be hung down in the well where the temperature was about 20 degrees cooler. No, we didn't have refrigeration in those days. There was no electricity in the community, and we couldn't afford ice for the ice box. Some people in modern times think they live a very deprived existence, but I have never known any of them to live without refrigeration or even a television set.

I was acutely aware of what difficulties my parents were having trying to keep clothes on our backs, food in our stomachs and meeting the mortgage payments on the farm. I thought surely there would be something I could do to help out. I had been observing my mother with her flock of Rhode Island Red hens, getting a few eggs along for cooking purposes and occasionally having some to sell to a poultry dealer in town. This provided her with a little "egg money" to buy mostly food staples and maybe a little left over to buy some material for a Sunday dress. Often she would say, "If I just had more eggs to sell." Then one day the answer came to me. I had heard about a neighbor lady who had gotten a start of a new breed of chickens called "Leghorns." They were an all-white, very excitable and fragile breed, but reputedly could lay an egg every day.

I immediately decided I wanted to start a flock of these exotic birds and went over to visit the neighbor lady to find out all about taking care of them. I had visions of having a big flock and gathering bucketfuls of beautiful white eggs every day. When I made inquiry about buying the baby chicks from a hatchery, I found them to be very expensive and completely out of reach of my finances. I rather sadly decided to give up the dream.

The neighbor lady, hearing of my disappointment, offered to sell me six of her birds which were about half-grown. She said if I took real good care of them and saved all the eggs the next spring, I could hatch out a whole flock. I jumped at the opportunity and shortly thereafter had my six young birds in a little house of their own, complete with roosting boards and egg-laying nests. I visited my little flock at least three times a day and never let them run out of feed and water.

After about six weeks and still a long way from egg laying, I went out early one morning to take care of them and, of course, look for eggs. Imagine my great surprise and joy to find two very small white eggs in the nest. I went racing back to the house with my find and proudly showed them to everyone. My big brother Harold, with a perfectly straight face, said, "They're kinda small, aren't they?" It was then that I realized they were about the size of my thumb and were a pretty poor excuse for a hen's egg. But I stoutly argued that my chickens weren't full-grown yet and would naturally lay little eggs to begin with. Finally it began to dawn on me that Harold had put those eggs in there and had gotten them from a pigeon nest in the barn.

I'm tempted to leave off the conclusion of this story because it had a sad ending. Just about the time my leghorns were old enough to start laying eggs, there was a disease that broke out in my mother's flock, and apparently sparrows going from one hen house to another carried the disease to my birds. My mother lost several of her hens, and I lost my entire flock. Probably my light-weight, more fragile birds were more susceptible to the disease and thus suffered greater mortality.

After that failure I began to look for other sources of income. During the winter months I could pick up a little loose change from selling wild rabbits at the local grocery store. I'm not sure just what use was made of the rabbits. Some people said they were shipped back east and fed to zoo animals, but I'm satisfied they were used for human consumption as well. We sometimes would dress a young wild rabbit for our own table and found it very good eating. Early in the winter season I would get paid 10¢ each for the rabbits I brought in, but later the price would fall to 8¢, and rifle shells cost 25¢ a box. I had to be sure to get a rabbit with each shot. Fortunately there seemed to be a never-ending supply of wild rabbits in our community, and I often had five or six to take to the store each week. As you can readily see, this did not make me rich, but with this income I could keep myself supplied with a good cheap Barlow pocket knife which was the mainstay of every red-blooded farm boy.

After my father had gotten started in his dairy enterprise, I decided I would like to own a calf of my own and maybe even start my own dairy herd. The first big hurdle was, of course, getting the money for purchase of the calf, but my father had started receiving money from the cream he sold and decided to encourage me by buying my first calf.

My calf was a beautiful purebred Guernsey heifer purchased from the same source in Wisconsin from which my father had gotten his start. There was concern about the disease that had afflicted my father's herd, but we had learned the disease would not spread to young stock if they were kept separated from older animals. I certainly wasn't going to take any chances with the disease in my herd, so I kept my calf well apart from the older herd.

I took such good care of my calf that it grew to be much larger than the average for the breed and showed promise of being a heavy milk producer. When she was about ready to have her first calf, we had a visitor, a total stranger to me,

103

who said he had heard about my prize heifer and wanted to see her. Of course, I proudly took him to see her. After looking her over carefully and feeling of her now swollen udder, he straightened up, looked me straight in the eye and said, "I'll give you a hundred dollars for her." I was completely stunned. I had no idea he was looking to buy, and I had no thought of ever selling her. I guess I didn't say anything for awhile because he finally turned to go and said over his shoulder, "If you decide to sell, let me know."

I didn't stop to analyze this situation but raced to find my father to tell him what had happened. I hadn't even thought about selling my calf, but one hundred dollars was an awful lot of money. My father didn't show any great amount of surprise at this disclosure and quietly said, "You can do a lot of things with a hundred dollars." I later suspected he had set the whole thing up with this man and had probably already come to a tentative agreement on the price. Needless to say, I finally succumbed to the lure of big money and let her go.

You might have thought after all the stories I told of deprivation and desires I would have gone on a big spending spree, but I had seen enough hardship in my family to realize the value of having a "nest egg." I'm sure my parents encouraged me in this, but I took the entire amount and put it into a bank account for future use.

This sudden wealth didn't mean the depression was over for me. There were several more years of trying times, and eventually I suffered along with almost everyone else when the bank closed its doors and wiped out my savings. Fortunately I had already put most of my nest egg to good use, and when the bank closed I had very little to lose. My further experiences in financial undertakings will be related in the next chapter.

Chapter VIII

Getting Out into the Real World

SINCE WE LIVED approximately 10 miles from the nearest town and had to travel principally by horse-drawn vehicles, we seldom got out of our little church-oriented community. My sphere of activities, until I was ready for high school, was almost entirely within a one-mile radius of our house. If I ever got any farther than that, I had a morbid fear of not being able to find my way home. Of course, I traveled to town occasionally with my parents to be fitted with new shoes and a new suit when I outgrew them. Every other clothing item was ordered from a Sears and Roebuck catalog. But whenever we went outside of our community, I always stuck very close to my father for fear he would go off and leave me.

There were, however, a couple of times during my childhood when I did get away from home without my parents. The first time, I think I must have been about five or six years old, when my sister Minnie talked me into going home with her for four or five days. She and her husband Joe lived in the town of Hardin which was about 10 miles away. Joe was part owner and manager of a Ford garage, and he and Minnie always had a good car to drive. I was promised they would bring me back home if I didn't want to stay that long.

The first day at Minnie's I wouldn't go any farther than the front porch from which I could see lots of cars going by and townspeople visiting on the streets. The second day, at my sister's urging, I walked down to the corner of the block all by myself to visit Joe's garage. I was quite impressed with all the shiny new cars being serviced. Over in one corner of the garage was a big object covered with a huge tarpaulin. This seemed to be some deep, dark secret, but my brother-in-law said for me to go ahead and look. I lifted up one end of the tarp and saw the most fabulous automobile I had ever seen. It was a big black hearse which a local undertaker was keeping in the garage until needed for a funeral. All the men in the garage laughed when they saw me staring at it and told me that I wouldn't want to ride in that car. I was awestruck by such a magnificent machine and marveled at the wonders of the outside world.

My visit in Hardin was during the summer and the weather was quite hot. My sister suggested I might like to go get an ice cream cone. I had never had one, but I knew what they were and was overjoyed at the prospect. Minnie gave me a nickel and told me how to get to the store. It was just two blocks on down the street, but the trip itself was an adventure for me. By the time I got back the ice cream was all gone and I was ready for another. Finally Minnie gave me another nickel, and I raced off for a second cone. To me this was the utmost in elegant living.

Along about supper time I began to feel a bit unwell and didn't want anything to eat. A little later on I was vomiting and running off at the bowels. I was extremely sick all night and barely able to get around the next morning. Apparently I had picked up salmonella food poisoning from the ice cream or rather from the ice cream scoop which was kept stored in a container of warm milky water. This was my first experience of the hazards of urban living, and I was ready to go home. However, Minnie talked me in to staying another day when it would be more convenient to take me back.

The next evening I was looking out across the city park which was just across the street from my sister's house. I saw three boys playing around a cement-mixing vat. They were a year or two older than I, but I just had to go see what they were doing. Workmen that day had put water in the vat to keep the cement from setting up overnight, and the boys were taking turns working the big long-handled hoe in the sloppy mix-

ture as though they were mixing the cement.

When I came over and rather timidly stood watching, they immediately spotted me as a gullible rube. The boy with the big mixing hoe said to me, "Did you know there is a baby possum in there?" That, of course, perked my interest, and I moved over to have a look. Then he said, "Come on up to the end and watch real close while I pull the cement off of him." He began pulling the big hoe slowly toward him as I leaned over to look. Suddenly he gave the hoe a big push which sent the sloppy mess flying all over my face and clothes. The incident was hilarious to the three older boys, but to me it was an embarrassing situation for me to go back to my sister's house and explain why I was covered with grime.

The second time I had a chance to visit in an urban setting was when my sister Vera invited me to come stay with them a few days. They were living on a farm just out of the town of Hardin, and they had heard about a potato grower just south of town wanting to hire town kids to come pick up potatoes. My nephew Gwendle was going to go and wanted me to go along with him. Needless to say, I jumped at the opportunity to earn a little spending money.

We went out into the fields where at least a dozen other kids were waiting to start. We were each given a number of gunny sacks to fill. The potatoes had been plowed out with a special kind of plow that would scatter the potatoes out where they could be readily seen and picked up. The owner of the field started each of us on a separate row and told us he expected us to pick up every potato in our row, even those which might be covered with loose dirt. If he found any of us leaving any potatoes along our row, he would fire us.

Our pay was to be 11¢ per sack, and we all had visions of having a pocketful of money at the end of the day. We started out with great enthusiasm. Each sack would hold approximately two bushels of potatoes when full and weigh about 100 pounds. Trying to drag that heavy sack down the row with one hand while picking up potatoes and sifting through the dirt with the other was a hot, back-breaking job. When the sack was about half full, we had a bucket we would fill and run back and forth to the sack.

After we had gotten a good start down our rows, the owner of the patch went off to another field to plow up more potatoes. As we were toiling along, a big pot-bellied man dressed in a white shirt and Panama hat came over to where we were working. He loudly informed us he was the buyer of those potatoes, and he wanted us to quit picking up all those little potatoes. He was a big blustery fellow and went charging around among us like a slave master. What were we to do? The owner had threatened to fire us if we didn't pick up all the potatoes, and the buyer was threatening us bodily harm, if we didn't leave out the little potatoes. The town kids knew exactly what to do, so I followed their lead. They left the little potatoes in the row until the big fat blustery buyer found the sun too hot for him to stay with us and went back to town. As soon as he was gone, everyone ran back down the row with their buckets and picked up all the little ones they had left.

I can't remember how many potatoes I picked up that first day, but it wasn't nearly as many as I had anticipated. The next day I did even less because I was so stiff and sore I could hardly move. Many of the town kids didn't even show up. I guess I made about $3 from the two-day potato field experience which was at least somewhat better than the $1 per day I had received from a neighbor back home for helping him gather his corn.

My next big departure from the family nest was when I started to high school. The school was not very large as high schools go, but was a consolidation of five different grade schools in the neighboring communities. The high school was centrally located among those outlying grade schools, so naturally was called Central High School.

Del had already been in high school for three years by the time I was ready to start. He had been riding Old Charlie, the five-gaited saddle horse I told you about earlier. It was necessary to have some means of transportation to this school because of the distance, but Del was not about to let me ride behind him on Old Charlie. That would have been very degrading to an upperclassman. So a decision was made to get a two-wheeled cart and break Old Charlie to the cart. That way the two of us could have transportation to high school without Del suffering the indignity of having a minor sibling riding behind him on horseback.

We started breaking Old Charlie to the cart the summer before I was ready to start to high school. We had an old ramshackle cart around the farm we had used to haul drinking water to harvest hands with another horse. We experimented with this cart around inside of the barn lot and even out into the pastures. Old Charlie didn't like this business very much but didn't make any violent protest, just pranced around a lot.

One very wet, soggy afternoon I decided to try driving Old Charlie hitched to the cart out on one of the back roads. I figured the muddy roads would discourage him from trying to run away from me. There wasn't anyone along with me — I had more or less sneaked out on my own to try my hand at cart driving. I was soon out on the back road slogging along at a good clip for muddy roads.

There was a rather steep incline at one point in the road, right about the place a mule had tried to push Old Prince into a gully. As we started down that incline, the cart began to go faster than Charlie and started bumping him on the thighs. When Charlie tried to go faster to stay ahead of the cart, I pulled back on the lines very hard to slow him down, but when

I pulled back I had to brace my feet against the floor of the cart which caused it to be shoved even farther into Charlie's rear end. Then Charlie really got excited and started running full tilt with mud flying in every direction. Unfortunately the road ended within a short distance and one had to turn sharply either to the right or to the left. Charlie took the left turn at full gallop, easily making change in direction, but the cart and rider were not so fortunate. The top-heavy cart turned over, flinging me out of the road into a side ditch head first into soft mud and water. I managed to pull my head out of the mud in time to see Charlie disappearing over the hill with remaining parts of the harness still flapping along behind.

I hurriedly ran after the fleeing horse, disregarding any possibility of a broken neck or any other bones until I came to our schoolhouse. Charlie had turned into the school yard and had run through a partially downed fence. He was standing on the other side of the fence with a strand of barbed wire wrapped around one hind leg. Sweat was pouring off his body, and he was quivering with fear. The wire had cut deep gashes in his foot just above the hoof in the fetlock region, and blood was pouring out on the ground. I finally got the frightened animal quieted down sufficiently to remove the wire from his foot and led him limping home.

Charlie was several weeks recovering from the wound. Every time he would walk on that foot the sore would break open and start bleeding again. We finally had to tie him in his stall in the barn until healing was complete. Even then he was left with a big knot on that foot that remained with him the rest of his life.

School time came, and we started driving Charlie to another newer and more substantial cart. There were also some additions made to the harness to prevent the cart from running upon Charlie's rear end as it did with me. Charlie was always a very spirited horse and would take us flying along in the cart at what some considered breakneck speed. On our way to school we had to pass a little country grocery store, and the owner would hear us coming and run out on the front porch, wave his arms and yell us on as if we were in a race.

We had only one incident with Charlie and the cart that could have been serious. There was room for only two persons on the cart seat, so we couldn't take any other riders with us. However, there was one boy in school who kept pestering us to ride in the cart. He was the local preacher's son (my father had been replaced by an ordained minister) who had been reared in the city and thought it would be a great thrill to ride behind a fast horse. Finally after much nagging, we consented to let him ride the short distance to the parsonage which was on the road home for us.

Charlie was already hitched to the cart and anxious to go home after standing all day at the hitch rack. Our excited rider couldn't wait until Charlie was untied, but jumped up into the cart and grabbed the lines, which was a signal to Charlie that we were ready to go. Del had gone around to the head of the horse and had untied the hitch rein and was fastening it to the harness. I was just getting ready to get into the cart when our over-exuberant rider yelled, "Yea!" That was all it took for Charlie. He whirled and took off like a scalded dog, leaving both Del and me standing there with our mouths open. We quickly ran after the horse and cart, but by the time Charlie left the school yard he was going full tilt with the scared rider pulling back on the lines yelling, "Whoa! Whoa!" We ran futilely after him, fully expecting the horse to crash the cart into a fence or ditch, but Charlie was heading straight down the middle of the road at a full gallop.

At the bottom of the hill there was a cross road. Either the horse could go straight ahead or make a left turn which would be the way home. Naturally Charlie made the left turn, and one wheel of the cart went around on the edge of the bridge abutment just inches from a deep ditch. I can distinctly remember seeing that left wheel spinning in mid-air as it left the bridge abutment. Somehow the cart managed to right itself as the horse started up the next hill.

By this time Charlie began having second thoughts about what he was doing and maybe even remembered what kind of mess he got himself into before. Anyway he responded to the violent sawing of the bit in his mouth and came to a stop. Very shortly we caught up to the cart and Del got into the seat and ordered the rider out. He needed no further suggestion, and I took my place on the cart seat and we continued on home.

I can't recall that I accomplished much of anything during my freshman year. I guess I spent most of my time trying to adjust to a much larger group of people, and being of a timid nature I just sort of faded into the obscurity of the mob. There was, however, one achievement that stands out in my memory.

For some reason during that particular year the schoolhouse, the adjacent country store and various outbuildings were overrun with rats and mice. They were everywhere. Mice could be seen scurrying around in the classrooms during the day, and the rats hid out under the schoolhouse floor and came out at night to chew on anything resembling food. Even the glue on book bindings was fair game. The Home Economics teacher was frantic about little mouse pellets all over her work benches and under the cabinets where she kept her cooking equipment. There were no safe and effective poisons in those days to control rats and mice, so about the only control available was trapping.

The superintendent of the school was a very clever man

and soon came up with a plan of attack. His idea was to organize the freshman class into rival teams that would compete with one another to see who could catch the most rats and mice. There was to be some kind of prize at the conclusion of the contest. He asked for volunteers to be leaders of competitive teams. Now this was my chance to excel at something in my freshman year. Mice were my forte. I eagerly volunteered, and a classmate offered to be a second leader, and soon the class was divided into two groups which immediately went into caucus to lay plans.

The next day I think every freshman brought with him a mouse trap from home and some brought steel traps for rats. We spent the greater part of one morning setting out those traps with our team designation on each trap. Results were almost immediately evident. Within two or three days we had caught an unbelievable number of mice, but no rats. They were far too smart for us. My team was slightly ahead when the mouse population was down to a bare minimum.

The Home Economics teacher had been adamant about letting anyone put a trap in her cabinet where she might get her fingers caught when reaching for a pan. So I suggested an alternate plan of using a little box trap and catching the mice alive. I had seen plans for such a trap in a magazine and was anxious to try it. The scheme was to use a wooden chalk box, cut a hole in one end just big enough for a mouse to enter, and insert straight pins around the edge of the hole in such a way as to form a funnel-like entrance into the box. It was on the order of a fish trap. The mouse could slip through this funnel-like arrangement but couldn't get out without being impaled by one or more of those pins. To some, this may seem cruel but as in the old adage, "All's fair in love and war." And we were definitely at war with these mice.

Our first victim came during a class in Health Science being conducted in the Home Economics room. The teacher's droning voice was suddenly interrupted by shrieks and squeaks from under the sink. The teacher knew who had put that trap under there, and I was ordered to take it outside and dispose of that mouse. That was the one and only time I got to use my revolutionary new mousetrap.

As the trapping contest started coming to a finish, the opposing team suddenly began coming up with more mice. That was difficult to understand because we were just not catching mice around the school. I always did think, but couldn't prove, they were bringing dead mice from home. They won the contest, and we had to put on a party for them.

Oh yes, about the rats: I don't think we caught a single one, but for some strange reason, when the mice began to disappear the rats also began to diminish. I always believed they thought there was something sinister going on and didn't want to be around to find out what it was.

My sophomore year in high school was a bit more productive. Del had graduated and had gone off to college, and I had sole possession of Old Charlie. I could come and go as I wished just as long as I was around to help with the chores at home. There were a few school parties I was allowed to attend, but my transportation was still horseback, and this was not conducive to having dates with girls. I was still very shy in relation to girls and merely watched them out of the corner of my eye.

My chief interest this year was a course in vocational agriculture. This was the first year it was being taught in our school, and most of the boys in our school wanted to take the course. The teacher was a recent graduate of the University of Missouri, School of Agriculture, and to us farm kids he knew everything there was to know about farming.

Of course, this wasn't the only subject we had that year. There was history, English, health science and, of course, the hated mathematics which had to be endured before we had the afternoon free for vocational agriculture.

Our first year in vocational agriculture was all about raising livestock, and we were required to have our own livestock project at home to practice what we were taught.

The most practical project for most of the boys was a pig project, and that is what we concentrated on. Our instructor would take us on field trips in his new Chevrolet automobile and help us pick out our pigs. I decided I liked the Duroc breed and bought a purebred registered gilt (the technical name for an unbred female). I had to pay $60 for my gilt which took a big chunk out of my $100 savings account. But I optimistically figured I would soon multiply that many times when I sold the offspring from my gilt. The purchase agreement was that the seller would keep the gilt until she was safely with pig (bred), and then I could pick her up and bring her home.

In the meantime, I was required by the rules of the project to build a portable house for my gilt so she could be moved to clean surroundings where pigs had not been raised before. This was to avoid having the baby pigs get intestinal parasites and pig disease germs from the soil. This was an entirely new concept of raising pigs for me and my father. We had always required our sows to have their pigs in the same old permanent sheds and pens year after year. I felt very proud to have learned such important things.

Our vocational agriculture teacher was building a prototype of a farrowing house at school to show us how it should be done. We had to buy our own lumber and build the same type of structure at our own farms. I've forgotten how much the lumber cost, but it took another bite out of my savings account at the bank, but by this time I was so sure of my profits that I would have gladly spent the rest of my savings.

In a very few days my farrowing house was constructed and a fence built around a small area in the orchard. I was all ready when the seller of my gilt called to say she was ready to

be picked up. I was mighty proud of my pig project.

Five months later nature took its course, and 10 little baby pigs were born. I stayed with the new family almost night and day until all was going well. The pigs thrived throughout the following summer, and by the time school opened in the fall they were ready for sale.

Our teacher had arranged to have a breeders' sale for the best of our litters. Each boy was permitted to pick out three for the show and sale. The remaining pigs in the litter would be sold on the market for pork. That meant I would have seven pigs going to market.

Our show and sale did not fare too well. There were very few outside buyers, and the farmers in our community were not quite convinced that these high-powered purebreds would perform as well as their cross-bred stock under usual farm conditions. Besides, at that time market prices for hogs were not such as to encourage expansion of swine herds. My three pigs sold for $30 apiece, which was quite a letdown from my expectations. When I saw they were going so cheaply, I talked my father into buying one of the gilts back for me to keep for expanding my project.

When the rest of the litter was ready for market, I figured these should bring in quite a sum, but again I had a disappointment. In keeping with the rules of our project, we were required to keep account of all the feed we had used to raise our animals. Our instructor told us we should pay for all the feed we had used from our fathers' corn cribs, plus any he had bought for us from the feed store. This was to teach us the true facts of the pig business.

When I received my check from the meat packers, it was just barely enough to pay for the feed I had borrowed from my father. Since I had asked my father to buy one of my gilts for me, I had to repay him from the sale of the other two. In other words, my profit for the entire project was $30. For the first time I began to wonder about the wisdom of making a career out of farming.

During my junior year in high school I continued taking

vocational agriculture as my major subject, but I began to expand my interests into other areas as well. I came out for the basketball team and managed to become a "sub," which meant I could play if someone broke a leg or fouled out of the game. But as a substitute, I did get to travel with the team to the county seat for a basketball tournament in which we came out second in the county.

I also got to travel to the county seat as a member of the glee club which was one activity in which our school excelled. We nearly always came back with a trophy, largely because for several years we had a very talented and dedicated music teacher on the teaching staff. I also tried my hand at public speaking, entering a declamation contest wherein I delivered the Gettysburg address just as I thought Old Abe Lincoln would have done. I won first prize largely because there were only two contestants.

The line of study in vocational agriculture for this year was all about field crops. We had covered livestock management the previous year. Each student was required to plan and carry through on a grain crop as a project for the course. Since I needed a lot of corn to feed my increased hog business, I decided that corn should be my project.

There was a lot of study and preparation for this project. We learned that corn needed a lot of nitrogen to produce a big crop and, of course, we all wanted to try for that "Pie in the Sky" honor of producing 100 bushels per acre. We also studied how to select and test seed corn for germination (sprouting capability). There were no sources of hybrid seed corn available in those days, and we had to test our own.

Our only source of nitrogen in those days was livestock manure. Commercial fertilizers had not yet been promoted, and in those days of severe farm depression no one could afford them anyway. All winter long I faithfully cleaned out our horse and cow stables and hauled it to my little one-acre plot which my father had allocated to me. When spring plowing time came, I had a generous covering of manure on my acre to be plowed under.

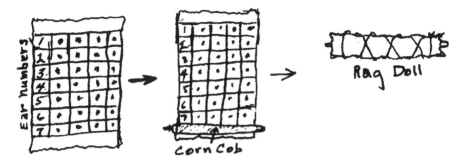

Ear numbers

Corn Cob

Rag Doll

To test for germination of our seed, we learned about the Rag Doll test. This consisted of taking a few grains from each of a number of ears of corn and placing them on a wet cloth marked off in little squares numbered to correspond to the ears of corn from which the grains had been taken. After it was all laid out, we would select a nice clean corn cob and carefully roll up the cloth and grain over the corn cob so as not to get the grains out of their squares. When the so-called Rag Doll was all wrapped up, it was loosely tied with twine, thoroughly wet down with warm water and placed in a warm spot in the kitchen. At the end of a week the rag doll could be carefully unwrapped to determine which ears of corn had good germination. To test every ear of corn to be used for planting an acre of corn would, of course, require a lot of rag dolls, and I spent a lot of time that winter testing the seed I was going to use.

In the spring I plowed my acre plot as early as possible and turned under all that good barnyard manure. I worked the ground with disk and harrow until it was in beautiful condition for planting. When the proper time came, I had my father do the planting because he could make the rows very straight with the corn planter, and I wanted him to plant twice as much seed in my rich soil to make that 100-bushel-per-acre honor.

The corn grew very rapidly through the warm days of June and was already taller than my head by the first of July. I was out there almost every day watching jealously for a weed to show up to be chopped out. My corn was at least two feet taller than my father's corn just across the fence.

Then around the 4th of July the weather became very hot

and dry. For the next four weeks we didn't have a drop of rain, and the winds became very hot and searing. The leaves on my lush stand of corn curled up and began to droop. The tassels just starting to form turned white with the heat and failed to fertilize the newly developing ears. The entire crop was a total failure. I didn't even get enough corn to replace the seed I had borrowed from my father.

Meanwhile, my father's puny corn across the fence was struggling along at a much slower pace but was managing to complete its biological cycle. My father was able to gather enough corn to provide feed for the livestock the following winter. I had learned a lesson that summer that had not been taught in my class in agriculture: an oversupply of nitrogen will cause a plant to grow too rapidly and thus make it more susceptible to drought.

I was absolutely devastated by this corn crop failure. After all the hard work and educated expertise, I came out with nothing. I vowed then and there I would get out of the farming business forever. There could be no future for me in a business as uncertain as this.

My senior year in high school was marked by a rather radical change in direction. I did not enroll in vocational agriculture partly because of my previous failures and partly because I felt I should prepare myself for college. Both of my brothers had managed to obtain college degrees, and I didn't want to be the only dummy in the family.

I began by signing up for difficult subjects such as physiology, higher mathematics, civil government and English and American literature. I plunged into my studies with some urgency, getting a smattering of algebra, geometry and even trigonometry. However, literature turned out to be my favorite subject. The course was taught by our school superintendent, and he had a way of making the literature come to life for me. I began reading books that I didn't even know existed before. My favorite author at that time was Mark Twain (Samuel Clemens). I liked his down-to-earth sense of humor as opposed to the more aloof, sometimes difficult to read, authors of Old

English literature.

I did very well in my subjects that year and might have done even better had I not fallen in love. I had suddenly discovered one of the most beautiful girls I had ever seen. It was her second year in high school, but somehow I hadn't been aware of her beauty until she began to blossom out. She had the most beautiful long auburn, almost golden, curls falling down around her shoulders and soft fawn-like eyes that would timidly peer out among the curls. It took me most of the school year to get up enough courage to ask here for a bonafide date, but all of the school kids knew we were "going steady" because of the way we would hang around each other during the noon hour and ride down the road together every evening on the way home from school.

It wasn't until after school was out for the summer that I asked her for a date to come sit on her front porch. I had to go on horseback since my father didn't think I was yet old enough to drive a car. I didn't get to stay very long on those dates because her mother would start clearing her throat about 9:30 which was a signal for me to go home.

The romance was rather short-lived. I had made arrangements along about mid-summer to come see her on a Sunday afternoon rather than the usual evening dates. I had ridden Old Charlie and was sitting around on the front porch playing with her little brother and sister. I noticed she was a little nervous that afternoon but didn't think much about it until a bright new sports roadster pulled up at the front gate. A well-dressed young man got out and started toward the house. It was then she admitted she had another date that afternoon and had forgotten I was coming. It was very embarrassing all the way around, but I decided I didn't have a chance to compete with a slick-looking dude with a sports car, so I got on Old Charlie and left for home. I couldn't blame her for choosing a sports car over a horse and besides, we both knew at that time I was going to be gone from the community for a long time. However, that didn't keep me from dreaming about her for many years to come.

Getting back to my senior days in high school, I would be remiss if I didn't tell about my experiences as a member of the debate team. I really don't know why I ever signed up for such an activity. I didn't enjoy public speaking and certainly had no particular talent for it. I suppose my reason was, as always, I had to do everything that Del did when he was in school. He had been on the debate team during his senior year and had won all of his debates. Those who had remembered his success thought surely I could do as well and used this tactic to pressure me to participate. I finally agreed to give it a try.

Our debate coach was the Home Economics teacher who had never had any training in this sort of thing but was required by the school superintendent to sponsor the activity. She acquired from state headquarters a kit of ready-made material on the subject that was selected for the year's debating schedule. Everything pertaining to the debate was all worked out, including the affirmative and the negative sides of the issue. They even had the rebuttals all planned. All we had to do was to memorize the entire packet of material and practice delivering it in a loud and authoritative manner. It was a good thing the subject matter was all written out for us because the topic was "Resolved that the Philippines should be given their Independence from the United States." I didn't even know we owned them nor where they were located, but we dutifully went ahead with memorizing both sides of the issue.

My teammate in this debate was a girl I had grown up with during my grade school days and was very talented in oral delivery of the material. We worked very hard at this for several weeks and finally felt we were ready for competition with other schools. Our first debate was with a team in a small town high school within our county. We were, of course, a bit apprehensive about our first time before an audience, but we managed to go through the entire debate without any noticeable mistakes. Even our rebuttals we had memorized fit very nicely because our opponents had used the state-prepared material just as we had.

After the debate was over, the official judges conferred and decided in our favor. Naturally we felt very good about this and talked excitedly all the way home. This win meant we would now go to the next highest bracket and debate the winners in the adjoining county.

A week later we were on our way to the next county to debate a team from a much larger school and presumably with a much better debating team. We were not greatly alarmed because we had already presented our material before an audience and had won a debate. We were confident we could do it again.

Both teams were on stage before a big audience, and the opposing team had the first presentation. According to the script we had all received from the state office, each speaker was to present two main points and spend five minutes proving each point, making a total of 10 minutes each person was to be on the floor.

The first opposing speaker rose to his feet, walked to the center of the stage and in a cultured voice said, "Honorable judges, worthy opponents, ladies and gentlemen: After much thought and consideration, we have decided to concede the first point of the debate to our honorable opponents because we feel there are better reasons for taking our position in this debate." He then proceeded to complete his arguments with an entirely different set of points than we had planned.

This turn of events was as devastating as if the roof had fallen on our heads, and I think we would have welcomed just such a calamity. Half of my debating time was geared to proving the point they had just conceded, and my partner's first five-minute rebuttal was designed to disprove what they had conceded. We felt as if we were way out on a limb, and it was being sawed off at the trunk. My partner kept whispering, "What are we going to do? What are we going to do?"

I was petrified, and sweat began to creep down across my face. What was I going to do with that part of my speech they had conceded? There was no way I could make up a new speech up there on the stage. I hardly heard a word my opponent was saying. I only wished I could slip out of there.

Suddenly it was my time to speak. I rose to my feet and felt certain my knees were going to buckle beneath me. I went trembling to center stage and gave the usual salutation, after which I rather lamely said I thought the point my worthy opponents had conceded was vitally important to debate and I was going to prove it. I then went on to recite my memorized speech. I hardly heard a word of what the second opposing speaker was saying, but he was using the same script we had memorized, so I knew my partner would be in line with her speech. I tried to concentrate on rewriting my rebuttal, but all I could think of was what a fool they had made of me. I felt deep resentment toward my coach and the school officials for getting me into this mess. Of course, my resentment should have been directed toward the coach of the opposing team for pulling this cheap, unethical trick. He knew full well we would be using the material sent out by the State Board of Education, and he rewrote the speeches of his debaters to throw us into confusion.

Of course, we lost the debate and I vowed I would never be caught in a situation like that again. I still suffer from that traumatic experience whenever I find myself in front of an audience in any kind of an extemporaneous situation.

Toward the end of my senior year I began thinking seriously about what I should plan to do after I graduated. I had just been through the sad experience with my corn-growing project and knew I certainly wasn't going to stay on the farm. My oldest brother Harold had gotten a degree in Agriculture at Oklahoma A & M College and was teaching vocational agriculture in a high school, and Del was well on his way toward a degree from Park College located north of Kansas City. They had both gone through some rather trying times to get that education because there was very little financial help from our folks.

As I said earlier, I was not a top notch student, and there was little hope of getting a scholarship as did Del when he started to college. However, I had shown considerable potential during my last year in high school and had managed to come out second highest in grade points in my class. The superintendent of our school liked my essays in literature and thought I should go on to college to further my education along these lines. He had attended a small church-oriented college, Westminster College in Fulton, Missouri, and felt this would be the ideal place for me. I was not of the same religious persuasion as was this school, but I was not about to train myself for the ministry anyway. I had already been approached on that score by a Dean of our own church school.

This Dean had come to our house unannounced one rainy Saturday afternoon to talk to me about entering his college. I was in the barn building a dog house. He caught me in a pair of old ragged bib overalls with my pant legs rolled up and barefooted with mud between my toes from wading around in the barn lot. I was so embarrassed for being caught in such a disreputable condition that I probably gave him rather short answers to his invitation to come to his school. Anyway he never came back to see me again.

My school superintendent kept urging me to consider Westminster College and even wrote their admissions dean about my qualifications. As a result of his letter, I was offered a scholarship that would cover most of the tuition to the college. Then I became quite interested and contacted a boy in our community who had attended Westminster College. I found out from him the approximate cost of room and board at the dormitory and the incidental fees. These were not excessive as college expenses run, but for someone who had only a couple of hundred dollars in assets and no other sources of income, these costs were insurmountable. My parents were still strapped by their obligations to the land bank and couldn't help financially. I was about to give up the whole idea when suddenly I had an inspiration. Why couldn't I take a couple of our milk cows down there and sell milk to pay my expenses. I had the experience of milking and caring for cows on our farm and felt competent in that area.

As soon as school was out, I called up the boy who had attended Westminster College and asked him if he would go with me to visit the college and talk to the officials of my plan.

He readily agreed, and shortly thereafter we were on our way in our recently purchased Model T Ford. My father had heard of this car being for sale by a spinster lady who had barely driven it during the 10 years she had owned it. The car was a bright black shiny 1920 model without any scratches, and I was getting to drive it. I guess my father figured I was now old enough to drive and he was willing to risk our new (10-year-old) automobile.

We toured the campus before approaching the college dignitaries and met some of the summer students staying in the dormitory. Some of them said, "Oh, boy, you're going to be bringing the old jalopy to school with you, aren't you?" I didn't dare tell them this was the one and only family car.

When we went into the administration building, there was only a lady registrar present. School was not in session, and none of the school officials were present. I had not thought to make an appointment. When I said I guess we had made a trip for nothing, the registrar said she thought the president of the college was at home right next door and we might go talk to him.

The president was a tall, dignified, scholarly looking gentleman but very kindly. He listened to my story, I suspect with considerable amazement and perhaps even amusement. He knew nothing about cows except that they gave milk, and for some green country kid to come wanting to sell milk to the dormitory must have been quite a surprise. But after a few minutes he broke into a smile and said, "I think it is an excellent idea." He even offered to let me keep the cows on the unused portion of the athletic field which was located across a creek just behind the college campus. He also promised that the dormitory would buy all the milk I could furnish from my two cows at the going price of 25¢ per gallon.

My friend and I immediately went down to the athletic field to look at the possibilities for handling the cows. Providence must have been watching over me because there was a little unused two-acre plot at the end of the athletic field through which ran a clear stream of water. There was even a little empty storage shed on the plot which could easily be converted into a milking shed.

Needless to say, I was a very excited boy when I returned home and told my parents what I had found. My father was glad to contribute two cows to the furtherance of my education. He had planned to cut down on his dairy operation anyway after all his help was gone.

A few days before school started I cashed in my pig project, bought some cow feed, some fencing materials and hired a trucker to haul it, along with my two cows and all my worldly possessions, to the college where I was to spend the next two years.

It wasn't all roses. Some of the trials and tribulations I experienced would fill a small volume. But again I say, "Providence was with me."

From the Pictorial Review

TAKES COWS TO COLLEGE—Or, rather, cows take him to college. Lacking funds, Donald Rodabaugh took two Jerseys to Westminster college, Fulton, Mo. College officials arranged for him to supply milk in payment for his tuition. (Kobel.)